GREAT WOMEN'S SPEECHES

This edition first published in 2021 by White Lion Publishing,
an imprint of The Quarto Group.
The Old Brewery, 6 Blundell Street
London, N7 9BH,
United Kingdom
www.QuartoKnows.com

First published in 2019 as So Here I Am
Text © 2019 Anna Russell
Illustrations © 2019 Camila Pinheiro

A catalogue record for this book is available from the British Library.

ISBN 978 0 7112 5585 2

10 9 8 7 6 5 4 3 2

Design by Isabel Eeles

Printed in China

GREAT WOMEN'S SPEECHES

EMPOWERING VOICES THAT ENGAGE AND INSPIRE

ANNA RUSSELL

Illustrated by
Camila Pinheiro

WHITE LION PUBLISHING

Contents

Introduction

'Can you think of a speech by a woman?'

That's the question I asked friends and colleagues, family members, former teachers and the occasional unsuspecting stranger, as I started research on this book.

'Can you think of a speech by a woman?' I'd frame it festively, like a trivia question, or a game you might play on a long car ride. It was not a test or a trick; I didn't know the answer. Often, after some thought, the names of a few women would surface, slowly, like bits of silver dredged from the ocean floor, and we'd quickly latch on to them. The details were hazy and difficult to make out; the experience was like straining to listen to a conversation being held behind a closed door. 'Didn't Sojourner Truth say something?' we'd ask ourselves, sheepishly. 'What was it that Virginia Woolf expressed so eloquently?' And 'Who was that righteous bonneted lady who made a declaration at Seneca Falls?'

In the history of women, many tangible things have been lost to us: posters and petitions; buttons and flyers; private letters and secret diaries; artwork and criticism and literature, appropriated or unsigned for centuries; and an untold number of scrawled lists recording household tasks, doctor's appointments, due dates, groceries and funerals. So perhaps it's not so surprising that women's speeches are hard to pin down. What, after all, happens to our words after we speak them? Are they scribbled on notepads and transcribed into articles and books? Do they lodge in someone's ear, and repeat themselves at quiet moments? Or do they somersault away from our mouths and fade into obscurity?

Early on, I worried that we would not be able to find enough speeches by women to fill a book. One weekend in May, I went to the Brooklyn Public Library and examined a shelf of speech anthologies with serious, reassuring titles: *The Penguin Book of Modern Speeches*, *The Penguin Book of Historic Speeches*, *American Speeches*, *Give Me Liberty*. This is a treasure trove, I thought. Yet inside the largest collection, *The World's Great Speeches: 292 Speeches from Pericles to Nelson Mandela* (Fourth Enlarged Edition), I found almost as many speeches by men about women, as speeches by women. Former US senator Chauncey

Mitchell Depew appeared with a speech titled 'Woman', the US Civil War officer Horace Porter had 'Woman!' and Mark Twain, in 1882, outdid them both with 'Woman, God Bless Her'. Of 292 speeches, eleven were actually given by women.

In her magnificent history of feminism, *The Feminist Promise: 1792 to the Present* (2010), Christine Stansell writes of the consequences of 'historical amnesia' for the women's movement; of feminism's tendency towards 'compulsive repetitions of old mistakes, old arguments, old quandaries'. It's as if each generation of women, I've sometimes thought, coming into their own, and finding the world not as they wished it to be, attacked the same problems as their mothers and grandmothers – and even their great-grandmothers – without knowing which tools worked and which failed: a kind of perpetual reinvention of the wheel. Often, a new generation has turned on an older one, and, eyes blazing, blamed them for not doing more, without understanding the constraints on those earlier women, who may have been radicals in their own time. How, I wondered, can we still be asking ourselves, after all this thought and stress and study, what it is to be a woman in the world?

From the library, I walked towards the Brooklyn Museum, where Judy Chicago's room-sized installation, *The Dinner Party*, completed in 1979, is the centrepiece of the Elizabeth A. Sackler Center for Feminist Art. Structured as an enormous triangular banquet table, there is an elaborate place setting for thirty-nine iconic women from throughout history and mythology: Virginia Woolf is there, as is Georgia O'Keeffe, Sacajawea, Sappho and Elizabeth I. Beneath the table, on a 'Heritage Floor', are ceramic tiles painted with the names of nearly one thousand additional women, some familiar, others obscure: Alice Paul, Carlota Matienzo, Florence Nightingale, Catherine II (The Great), Clare of Assisi, Hipparchia, Maria Luisa Sanchez, Rose Mooney, Teresa Villarreal. We don't always think of history in terms of physical space, but Chicago's piece suggests the difficult work of developing a canon – of deciding who gets a seat at the table.

In the 1970s, with Women's Studies programmes in colleges still in their infancy, Chicago and her researchers compiled their list of

women from haphazard sources, from second-hand books and library catalogues, and by asking each other: an extended network of intelligent, collaborative women (and some men). They were quite literally building the table. By the time I first visited the work, as a curious middle-school student with my parents, over two decades later, the women invited to sit seemed like obvious choices, even a tad *too* obvious, with reputations beyond dispute. However, the space accorded to women, at a table or in an exhibition or within an anthology, is never without dispute. These are not academic questions: it took some twenty-two years, despite sold-out shows around the world, for *The Dinner Party* to find a permanent home in a museum.

The transmission of stories about women's lives and choices from one generation to the next is nothing new. It seems likely women have always done it, in private spaces among one another, in gossip or whispered phrases or unsigned work. (In the 1929 essay *'A Room of One's Own'*, Virginia Woolf supposes that '... Anon, who wrote so many poems without signing them, was often a woman.') Around the time of the French Revolution, women began grappling with the state of their political lives in print; as the British intellectual Mary Wollstonecraft did in *A Vindication of the Rights of Woman* (1792), and as Olympe de Gouges, the French activist and playwright, did in her 'Declaration of the Rights of Woman and the Female Citizen' (1791). These were powerful and clear-eyed tracts about women's lot in life; forthright about changes that needed to be made. Still, they were written rather than spoken. The public sphere in many cultures, where lectures and debates took place, was a space reserved almost exclusively for men. At last, in the early 1800s, women, particularly in the United States and the United Kingdom, began speaking out in public about their own condition.

This was a revolutionary act; eggs were thrown, reputations were ruined. In 1829, when the Scottish-born abolitionist Fanny Wright gave an American lecture tour on subjects as innocuous as the importance of education before audiences of both men and women, she was met with scorn, denounced as a prostitute and called a 'red harlot of infidelity'.

Many of the early speeches in this collection come from female abolitionists in the United States, who, speaking out against slavery, soon came to question their own status as second-class citizens. Maria Stewart, an African-American abolitionist, spoke courageously about women's potential as early as 1832. Angelina and Sarah Grimké, the daughters of Southern plantation owners, scandalized their family when they embarked on an anti-slavery speaking tour. In 1838, Angelina gave a passionate speech at Pennsylvania Hall, while an angry mob battered at the doors, and later burned the place down.

This book was a collaborative project. It would not have been completed without a team of fantastic editors working tirelessly to contact foundations, estates, literary agents and archivists to secure the rights for each of the speeches, brought beautifully to life by Camila Pinheiro's incandescent illustrations, with essential fact checking by Helene Remiszewska. Once I dug into the research, I found my fears about filling the book entirely unfounded. I sent out a wider call for suggestions, from historians, journalists, Women's Studies professors, and more friends. The recommendations soon came pouring in, often for a specific speech but sometimes simply for a pioneering woman. One name inevitably led to another, and before we knew it the floodgates had opened and we had more speeches than we could handle. And what gems! There was Victoria Woodhull, in a strikingly modern speech from 1871, declaring her allegiance to the principles of free love ('Yes, I am a Free Lover' she shouted). There was Nellie McClung, the Canadian suffragette, who hosted a sharply funny 'Mock Parliament' in 1914, in which women debated giving *men* the right to vote. There was Simone Veil, in 1974, with an eloquent and empathetic case for legalising abortion in France, delivered before a room filled almost entirely with men. In 2012 Manal al-Sharif courageously recounted for an audience in Oslo how she flouted a ban on women driving in Saudi Arabia, and galvanized a movement (losing her job and her home in the process). Elizabeth Cady Stanton, the American suffragette who read the 'Declaration of Sentiments' at the Seneca Falls Convention in New York, inquired beautifully in her 1892 speech

'The Solitude of Self', 'Who, I ask you, can take, dare take, on himself the rights, the duties, the responsibilities of another human soul?'

This volume begins in the early nineteenth century (save for Elizabeth I's speech on the Spanish Armada to her troops at Tilbury, which comes to us like a distant rallying cry) and carries forward into the present. Public speeches are often tied to activism; accordingly, the speeches in this book are windows into broad social and political movements, from suffrage to civil rights, to LGBTQ equality and proactive environmental policy. They dip elegantly into the arts: Toni Morrison dazzles on storytelling in her Nobel Prize acceptance speech, structured as a deceptively simple parable about an old woman and a bird. Maya Lin, in a commencement address, asks a graduating class of art students to consider, 'How will your works be read and felt one hundred years from today?' J.K. Rowling, in all respects the opposite of a failure, extols the benefits of defeat: 'Failure taught me things about myself that I could have learned no other way.' They are by turns witty, persuasive, personal, uncompromising and passionate. Often they are addressing other women on that thorny, perennial question: How should a woman be?

Like all anthologies, this one is incomplete – by no means definitive. Inevitably, we have had to limit our scope and leave some fantastic women for the next collection. Most of the speeches here were originally given in English, and many come from the United States and the United Kingdom, where vocal women's movements began early on. But there are representatives as well from other countries including France, Australia, Kenya, Liberia, Egypt, Pakistan, Poland and more. Sometimes, we desperately wanted to include a particular woman but were stymied when it came to securing a reliable speech text. Most of the speeches appear within these pages in excerpted form, but they are all worth looking up in their entirety. It is my hope that readers might take these entries and illustrations as a jumping-off point: a springboard to further discoveries.

One additional note: the women you will find in this collection are not heroines or saints, however much we might wish for them

to be. They are, or were, real people, often politicians, engaged in compromise and blunder and difficult decisions. Sometimes I found troubling contradictions, as with some of the early suffragettes' fraught relationship with race, or with some of Margaret Sanger's problematic, and even eugenicist, approaches to birth control. Heads of state, like Indira Gandhi and Margaret Thatcher for example, often leave complicated legacies as well. Yet, the speeches included here are ones that moved and inspired, that captured a particular moment and crystallized for successive generations its frustrations and aspirations. These are speeches that started revolutions, both the kind that take place in the public square – in mass demonstrations and violent clashes – and the quieter kind, which take place in the mind. These are speeches that should be remembered.

Furthermore they build on one another. One fascinating discovery that comes from reading so many brilliant speeches at once is the connective threads that emerge. In 2014, when the British actress Emma Watson spoke at the United Nations about ending gender inequality, she referenced a speech made by Hillary Clinton in Beijing in 1995, in which Clinton declared, famously, 'women's rights are human rights once and for all'. Clinton, in her own speech, described the long wait women in the United States faced before they won the vote, a movement formally set in motion, perhaps, when Elizabeth Cady Stanton stood to read the 'Declaration of Sentiments' in 1848. Ruth Bader Ginsburg, in a sweeping argument before the Supreme Court in 1973, quoted the abolitionist Sarah Grimké, Angelina's sister: 'I ask no favor for my sex. All I ask of our brethren is that they take their feet off our necks.' Alicia Garza, one of the founders of Black Lives Matter, paid homage to Sojourner Truth and Ida B. Wells in her 'Ode to Black Women'. In 1992, the writer Naomi Wolf called up Virginia Woolf's 'Professions for Women' speech, from 1931, in which she warned of the perils of self-censorship. The imaginative novelist Ursula K. Le Guin, in 'A Left-Handed Commencement Address', encourages women to look 'around and down,' among each other for inspiration. Many of the women in this collection learned from each other, and we can learn from them.

Elizabeth I
Queen of England (1558–1603)

Elizabeth I ascended to the English throne in 1558, when she was twenty-five, and ruled for the next forty-four years. Wary of marriage, she turned down a succession of suitors and was soon hailed 'The Virgin Queen', a nickname that played on her reputation as incorruptible, invincible and loyal, always, to England. Having succeeded her Roman Catholic half-sister, Mary I, Elizabeth was constantly on guard against a Catholic uprising that would challenge her power. When the Spanish Armada, a fleet of ships sent by Mary I's widowed husband, King Philip II of Spain, prepared for an invasion in 1588, England's troops gathered at Tilbury Camp. Many historians believe Elizabeth went among them on horseback (some say she wore a silver breastplate over a flowing white dress in reference, perhaps, to Edmund Spenser's epic poem *The Faerie Queene*).

If Elizabeth's speech was designed to unite and inspire the soldiers before battle, it was also a declaration of power. As a female ruler in a political sphere long dominated by men, Elizabeth used the language of war to both rally her troops and underscore her divine right to lead. She is there, she tells her listeners, not for 'recreation and disport', but 'to live and die amongst you all'. She draws explicit attention to her physicality, in order to differentiate it from what she sees as a more masculine spirit. She places herself in a position of both self-sacrifice and unquestionable power: 'I myself will take up arms,' she says, 'I myself will be your general, judge, and rewarder of every one of your virtues in the field.'

On the Spanish Armada 1588

We have been persuaded by some that are careful of our safety, to take heed how we commit our selves to armed multitudes, for fear of treachery; but I assure you I do not desire to live to distrust my faithful and loving people. Let tyrants fear. I have always so behaved myself that, under God, I have placed my chiefest strength and safeguard in the loyal hearts and good-will of my subjects; and therefore I am come amongst you, as you see, at this time, not for my recreation and disport, but being resolved, in the midst and heat of the battle, to live and die amongst you all; to lay down for my God, and for my kingdom, and my people, my honour and my blood, even in the dust.

I know I have the body but of a weak and feeble woman; but I have the heart and stomach of a king, and of a king of England too, and think foul scorn that any prince of Europe, should dare to invade the borders of my realm: to which rather than any dishonour shall grow by me, I myself will take up arms...

I know already, for your forwardness you have deserved rewards and crowns; and We do assure you in the word of a prince, they shall be duly paid you. In the mean time, my lieutenant general shall be in my stead, than whom never prince commanded a more noble or worthy subject; not doubting but by your obedience to my general, by your concord in the camp, and your valour in the field, we shall shortly have a famous victory over those enemies of my God, of my kingdom, and of my people.

Fanny Wright
Social Reformer

In 1829, the Scottish-born abolitionist Frances Wright (widely known as Fanny Wright) embarked on a lecture tour across the United States of America. The breadth and depth of her speeches, whose topics included slavery, children's rights, women's rights and intellectual freedom, was astounding. Wright, however, is not remembered so much for what she said, as for the fact that she said it before an audience that included both men and women – then called a 'promiscuous audience'. She was not rewarded for it. Critics called her a prostitute and the 'red harlot of infidelity', who wanted to make the world 'one vast immeasurable brothel'.

Yet Wright had her supporters. She was close to the Marquis de Lafayette, the military leader who played a key role in both the American and French revolutions, and corresponded with American founding father Thomas Jefferson. In a lecture series entitled 'On the Nature of Knowledge and Kindred Inquiries', she notes her unusual position. 'Perhaps at this moment, she who speaks is outraging a prejudice,' she told her audience. 'I should be tempted to ask, whether truth had any sex.' The condition of a society's women, she maintains, reflects the health of that society as a whole. She goes on to argue that the ideals of the United States – as she sees them, liberty and equality – include education for all. 'I have been led to consider the growth of knowledge, and the equal distribution of knowledge, as the best – may I say the only means for reforming the condition of mankind.'

Of Free Inquiry, Considered as a Means for Obtaining Just Knowledge 1829

However novel it may appear, I shall venture the assertion that until women assume the place in society which good sense and good feeling alike assign to them, human improvement must advance but feebly.... Let women stand where they may in the scale of improvement, their position decides that of the race.... that we could learn that what is ruinous to some is injurious to all....

There is a vulgar persuasion that the ignorance of women, by favouring their subordination, ensures their utility.... Surely it must have been a misconception of the nature of knowledge which could alone bring it into suspicion. What is the danger of truth? Where is the danger of fact? Error and ignorance, indeed, are full of danger. They fill our imagination with terrors. They place us at the mercy of every external circumstance. They incapacitate us for our duties as members of the human family, for happiness as sentient beings, for improvements as reasoning beings. Let us awake from this illusion. Let us understand what knowledge is. Let us clearly perceive that accurate knowledge regards all equally; that truth or fact is the same thing for all humankind; that there are not truths for the rich and truths for the poor, truths for men and truths for women; there are simply truths, that is, facts, which all who open their eyes and their ears and their understandings can perceive.

Maria Stewart
Journalist and Abolitionist

The African-American abolitionist Maria Stewart's
extraordinary career made her a woman of firsts. Widely
considered the first American woman to lecture before a
mixed-gender audience, she was also one of the first to
speak publicly on the role of women in society. Decades
before the Civil War, and long before the term
'intersectionality', Stewart was one of the first to speak
about the lived experience of African-American women.

Stewart was an unlikely public figure. Orphaned as a
child and an indentured servant from the age of five, she
received almost no formal education. Yet she was
passionate about civil rights and social reform. In 1831, as a
young widow, she sought out the abolitionist William Lloyd
Garrison, who quickly published an essay of hers on race
and religion in his newspaper, *The Liberator*. After this,
Stewart's popularity grew, and she gave four high-profile
anti-slavery lectures in Boston, until, facing increasing
criticism, she swore off public speaking in 1833 and retired
to life as an educator.

In her 'Farewell Address', Stewart namechecks powerful
women who came before her (she found their stories in an
old history book, *Sketches of the Fair Sex*, from 1790).
Deeply religious, she is confident that St. Paul, if only given
the chance to consider her life, would understand her
need to speak in public. She asks a simple question:
'What if I am a woman?'.

Farewell Address 1833

What if I am a woman; is not the God of ancient times the God to these modern days? Did he not raise up Deborah to be a mother and judge in Israel? Did not Queen Esther save the lives of the Jews? And Mary Magdalene first declare the resurrection of Christ from the dead?... St. Paul declared that it was a shame for a woman to speak in public, yet our great High Priest and Advocate did not condemn the woman for a more notorious offense than this; neither will he condemn this worthless worm. The bruised reed he will not break, and the smoking flax he will not quench till he send forth judgment unto victory. Did St. Paul but know of our wrongs and deprivations, I presume he would make no objection to our pleading in public for our rights.

... If such women as are here described have once existed, be no longer astonished, then, my brethren and friends, that God at this eventful period should raise up your own females to strive by their example, both in public and private, to assist those who are endeavoring to stop the strong current of prejudice that flows so profusely against us at present. No longer ridicule their efforts, it will be counted for sin. For God makes use of feeble means sometimes to bring about his most exalted purposes.

In the fifteenth century, the general spirit of this period is worthy of observation. We might then have seen women preaching and mixing themselves in controversies. Women occupying the chairs of Philosophy and Justice; women haranguing in Latin before the Pope; women writing in Greek and studying in Hebrew; nuns were poetesses and women of quality divines; and young girls who had studied eloquence would, with the sweetest countenances and the most plaintiff voices, pathetically exhort the Pope and the Christian princes to declare war against the Turks. Women in those days devoted their leisure hours to contemplation and study. The religious spirit which has animated women in all ages showed itself at this time. It has made them, by turns, martyrs, apostles, warriors, and concluded in making them divines and scholars.

Why cannot a religious spirit animate us now? Why cannot we become divines and scholars?...

What if such women as are here described should rise among our sable race? And it is not impossible; for it is not the color of the skin that makes the man or the woman, but the principle formed in the soul. Brilliant wit will shine, come from whence it will; and genius and talent will not hide the brightness of its lustre.

...it is not the color
of the skin that makes
the man or the woman,
but the principle formed
in the soul.

Maria Stewart

Angelina Grimké
Political Activist

The devout Angelina Grimké, daughter of prosperous South Carolina slaveholders, scandalized her family when she began an anti-slavery lecture tour in the 1830s. Even her close abolitionist friends, including her future husband, Theodore Weld, urged her to stop speaking publicly, fearing the spectacle of a woman addressing an audience would hurt the cause. The leading abolitionists were men, and Grimké's speeches, along with her sister Sarah's talks and writings, ventured into threatening territory by positioning women as the moral equals of men. In response to the situation, an uncomfortable New England church association issued 'The Pastoral Letter' to be read at services, reminding listeners that 'the power of woman is her dependence'.

Still, Grimké took the stage. She often named her faith as a source of strength in the face of others' disdain. In 1838 she addressed a mixed-race audience at Pennsylvania Hall, in downtown Philadelphia, where female abolitionist groups were holding a national convention. Outside, a violent mob battered at the doors and windows as she spoke. In her speech, she urges her audience, especially women, to use their right to petition (they did not yet have the vote) and to stand firm against angry voices, such as the mob's. (The bracketed comments in the extract opposite, describing the violence, were published along with the speech). Later, the crowd burned the empty building to the ground.

Anti-Slavery Speech 1838

As a Southerner I feel that it is my duty to stand up here to-night and bear testimony against slavery. I have seen it.... I know it has horrors that can never be described.... [Just then stones were thrown at the windows – a great noise without, and commotion within.] What is a mob? What would the breaking of every window be? What would the levelling of this Hall be? Any evidence that we are wrong, or that slavery is a good and wholesome institution?...

We often hear the question asked, 'What shall we do?' Here is an opportunity for doing something now. Every man and every woman present may do something by showing that we fear not a mob, and, in the midst of threatenings and revilings, by opening our mouths for the dumb and pleading the cause of those who are ready to perish.

...Women of Philadelphia! Especially let me urge you to petition. Men may settle this and other questions at the ballot-box, but you have no such right; it is only through petitions that you can reach the Legislature....

When the women of these States send up to Congress such a petition, our legislators will arise as did those of England, and say, 'When all the maids and matrons of the land are knocking at our doors we must legislate.' Let the zeal and love, the faith and works of our English sisters quicken ours – that while the slaves continue to suffer, and when they shout deliverance, we may feel the satisfaction of having done what we could.

Sojourner Truth
Abolitionist and Women's Rights Activist

Sojourner Truth's transformation from a slave in rural New York to a sharp-tongued, charismatic speaker, able to mesmerize and charm, is well-known. Born into a Dutch-speaking household around 1797, she was sold away from her family at about the age of nine. Two decades later, around the time slavery was outlawed in New York, she escaped her master's property. She later sued, successfully, for her son Peter's freedom.

In 1843, she had a spiritual awakening and changed her name to Sojourner Truth. She began delivering anti-slavery sermons, bolstered by sales of her memoir, *Narrative of Sojourner Truth: A Northern Slave*, which she wrote by dictation (Truth could neither read nor write). In 1851, at the Ohio Women's Rights Convention, she delivered her most famous speech, 'Ain't I A Woman?' She made a lasting impression, and several versions of her words have circulated over the years. The one reprinted most often, which became a touchstone for feminists and civil rights activists, was recorded from memory by the white abolitionist Frances Gage in 1863, twelve years after the original speech. Gage gave Truth, a born New Yorker, a misplaced Southern dialect. Some historians have also suggested that Gage introduced the phrase 'Ar'nt I a Woman?', later written as 'Ain't I A Woman?' Reproduced here is a version recorded closer to the time by the Reverend Marius Robinson, a friend of Truth's. Published in the newspaper *The Anti-Slavery Bugle*, it likely provides a more accurate rendering of Truth's extraordinary voice.

Ain't I A Woman? 1851

I want to say a few words about this matter. I am a woman's rights. I have as much muscle as any man, and can do as much work as any man. I have plowed and reaped and husked and chopped and mowed, and can any man do more than that? I have heard much about the sexes being equal; I can carry as much as any man, and can eat as much too, if I can get it. I am as strong as any man that is now. As for intellect, all I can say is, if woman have a pint and man a quart—why can't she have her little pint full? You need not be afraid to give us our rights for fear we will take too much,—for we can't take more than our pint'll hold. The poor men seem to be all in confusion, and don't know what to do. Why children, if you have woman's rights, give it to her and you will feel better. You will have your own rights, and they won't be so much trouble. I can't read, but I can hear. I have heard the Bible and have learned that Eve caused man to sin. Well if woman upset the world, do give her a chance to set it right side up again. The Lady has spoken about Jesus, how he never spurned woman from him, and she was right.... And how came Jesus into the world? Through God who created him and woman who bore him. Man, where is your part? But the women are coming up blessed be God and a few of the men are coming up with them. But man is in a tight place, the poor slave is on him, woman is coming on him, and he is surely between a hawk and a buzzard.

Victoria Woodhull
Social Reformer

Victoria Woodhull arrived in New York in 1868, and almost immediately created a sensation. In 1870, she and her sister, Tennessee Claflin, became two of the first female stockbrokers; the same year they started a newspaper.

In Woodhull's early years, she had worked as a clairvoyant as part of her family's shop. In this capacity, she later said, she heard from 'thousands of desolate, heart-broken men, as well as women', thwarted in love or trapped in bad marriages, who had come for advice. She developed a belief that the institution of marriage was at the heart of the problem. She became a vocal supporter of free love, which she defined as the ability to enter or exit a monogamous romantic relationship at will. The law had no place in love, she argued, especially in the context of marriage and divorce laws, which favoured men.

In 1871, a year before she became the first woman to run for President of the United States, she addressed an audience of 3,000 on this topic at Steinway Hall, New York City. She quoted the doctrine of free love as: 'The love that I cannot command is not mine; let me not disturb myself about it, nor attempt to filch it from its rightful owner...Rather let me leave my doors and windows open, intent only on living so nobly that the best cannot fail to be drawn to me by an irresistible attraction.' A mesmerizing speaker, Woodhull seems to have carried her audience along easily until, being challenged by a critic, she tore a white rose from her lapel and threw it down, declaring, 'Yes, I am a Free Lover'.

The Principles of Social Freedom 1871

Law cannot change what nature has already determined. Neither will love obey if law command. Law cannot compel two to love. It has nothing to do either with love or with its absence. Love is superior to all law, and so also is hate, indifference, disgust and all other human sentiments which are evoked in the relations of the sexes. It legitimately and logically follows, if love have anything to do with marriage, that law has nothing to do with it. And on the contrary, if law have anything to do with marriage, that love has nothing to do with it. And there is no escaping the deduction.

If the test of the rights of the individual be applied to determine which of these propositions is the true one, what will be the result?

Two persons, a male and a female, meet, and are drawn together by a mutual attraction – a natural feeling unconsciously arising within their natures of which neither has any control – which is denominated love. This [is] a matter that concerns these two, and no other living soul has any human right to say aye, yes or no, since it is a matter in which none except the two have any right to be involved, and from which it is the duty of these two to exclude every other person, since no one can love for another or determine why another loves.

... To love is a right higher than Constitutions or laws. It is a right which Constitutions and laws can neither give nor take, and with which they have nothing whatever to do, since in its very nature it is forever independent of both Constitutions and laws, and exists – comes and goes – in spite of them. Governments might just as well assume to determine how people shall exercise their right to think or to say that they shall not think at all, as to assume to determine that they shall not love, or how they may love, or that they shall love.

... And to those who denounce me for this I reply: Yes, I am a Free Lover. I have an inalienable, constitutional and natural right to love whom I may, to love as long or as short a period as I can; to change that love every day if I please, and with that right neither you nor any law you can frame have any right to interfere. And I have the further right to demand a free and unrestricted exercise of that right, and it is your duty not only to accord it, but, as a community, to see that I am protected in it. I trust that I am fully understood, for I mean just that, and nothing less!

To love is a right **higher** than Constitutions or laws.

Victoria Woodhull

Sarah Winnemucca
Author and Activist

When Sarah Winnemucca appeared before an Indian Affairs committee in the US House of Representatives in 1884, she became the first Native American woman to address Congress. Her speech drew on years spent advocating for her people, the Northern Paiutes. During the Bannock War, in 1878, she served as an interpreter, running messages between the US military and the Bannock people. After the war, in retaliation for the participation of a few Northern Paiutes, Winnemucca's people were forced on to the harsh Yakama Reservation, in what is now Washington State, where they suffered from illness, starvation and a lack of resources. In 1884, having tried and failed once to have her people released, Winnemucca took a petition to Washington, D.C.

Winnemucca was a gifted orator. Her Congressional testimony came on the heels of an extensive lecture tour, in which she gave speeches at venues up and down the East Coast. Years earlier, in San Francisco, she and her father gave dramatic talks on the plight of the Paiutes, in which she presented herself as an 'Indian Princess'. Snippets of her speeches exist in her autobiography, *Life Among the Piutes: Their Wrongs and Claims*, the first by a Native American woman. By all accounts, she was a mesmerizing speaker. 'The lecture was unlike anything ever before heard in the civilized world – eloquent, pathetic, tragical at times,' one reporter wrote, in 1879. '[Her] quaint anecdotes, sarcasms, and wonderful mimicry surprised the audience again and again into bursts of laughter and rounds of applause.'

Indian Affairs Statement 1884

But here came an order from the President to 'take all the five hundred Piutes under your care there and take them across the Blue Mountains, and across the Columbia River, to Yakama Reservation'.

This order came in December. Imagine what a severe winter it is out there at that time. They could not disobey the order although everything was said that could be in our behalf. But we took up the march and the soldiers had good buffalo shoes and buffalo robes and prepared for their comfort, and here were my people. They were poor and had no clothing and no blankets and no buffalo robes, and nothing to make them warm, because we did not belong to a buffalo country. We took up our march and marched over drifting snow, my people carrying their little children. Well it took us a good while. Some times, after we camped here and there, some would come along making a great noise crying. Some white people would mimic and mock them. Women would be coming along crying, and it was not because they were cold, for they were used to the cold. It was not because they were sick, for they suffered a great deal. The women were crying because they were carrying their little frozen children in their arms....

My people's dead bodies were strung all along the road across the Columbia River to this Yakama Reservation. When we got there we were turned over to another man, and then after we got there we died off like a lot of beasts, and of course then the following winter I came right here to Washington. I began to lecture about it in San Fransisco, and they sent for me and my father, the President did. We came on here and I pleaded - at least my father did - and of course my father asked for that same reservation back again. Says he 'I did not do anything'. He said 'my people did not do anything'. He said that our people had saved the lives of white people, and were now scattered everywhere and why should my people be punished like that?...

So you see they could not get back. How could any one get back to a place where they wanted to go and were not permitted to go while the lion was lying there with his mouth open ready to shut his teeth down upon them if they made the attempt?... So we have no reservation, no home and now I ask you for my people to restore us and put us I do not care where as long as it is in our own home, in the home where we were born, and that is all.

... I ask you for my people to restore us and put us I do not care where as long as it is in our own home...

Sarah Winnemucca

Elizabeth Cady Stanton
Suffragist

When Elizabeth Cady Stanton delivered her resignation speech, 'The Solitude of Self', in 1892, in her late seventies, it was with the weight of an adult life spent in the public eye crusading for women. Nearly a half-century earlier, in 1848, Stanton had submitted the 'Declaration of Sentiments' at New York's Seneca Falls convention – often called the birthplace of the organized women's movement in the United States. The Sentiments called for increased property, marriage and suffrage rights for women. Playing on the language in the 'Declaration of Independence', it announced, 'We hold these truths to be self-evident; that all men and women are created equal'.

Stanton spent much of the intervening five decades on the road, often with her close collaborator Susan B. Anthony, speaking, writing and organizing groups of women. She fought for temperance and abolition, but her great gift was shaping the early women's movement. More broad-minded than Anthony, she wanted to see equality across the board, beyond just the vote. In 'The Solitude of Self', which she gave on stepping down as President of the National American Woman Suffrage Association, Stanton offered a moving distillation of a lifetime of thought on women's place in society. Stanton's women are adventurers and independent beings, in the care of their own conscience and responsible, in the darkest hour, for their own souls. Although Stanton did not live to see American women gain the vote in 1920, her speech laid the foundation for a modern understanding of the female sex and gestured towards a new era in feminist thought. Expansive, poetic and deeply felt, Stanton's rhetoric soars.

The Solitude of Self 1892

The strongest reason for giving woman all the opportunities for higher education, for the full development of her faculties, forces of mind and body; for giving her the most enlarged freedom of thought and action; a complete emancipation from all forms of bondage, of custom, dependence, superstition; from all the crippling influences of fear, is the solitude and personal responsibility of her own individual life. The strongest reason why we ask for woman a voice in the government under which she lives ... is because of her birthright to self-sovereignty; because, as an individual, she must rely on herself. No matter how much women prefer to lean, to be protected and supported, nor how much men desire to have them do so, they must make the voyage of life alone, and for safety in an emergency they must know something of the laws of navigation. To guide our own craft, we must be captain, pilot, engineer; with chart and compass to stand at the wheel; to watch the winds and waves and know when to take in the sail, and to read the signs in the firmament over all. It matters not whether the solitary voyager is man or woman. Nature, having endowed them equally, leaves them to their own skill and judgment in the hour of danger, and, if not equal to the occasion, alike they perish.

To appreciate the importance of fitting every human soul for independent action, think for a moment of the immeasurable solitude of self. We come into the world alone, unlike all who have gone before us; we leave it alone under circumstances peculiar to ourselves. No mortal ever has been, no mortal ever will be like the soul just launched on the sea of life....

Inasmuch, then, as woman shares equally the joys and sorrows of time and eternity, is it not the height of presumption in man to propose to represent her at the ballot box and the throne of grace, to do her voting in the state, her praying in the church, and to assume the position of high priest at the family altar?...

The talk of sheltering woman from the fierce storms of life is the sheerest mockery, for they beat on her from every point of the compass, just as they do on man, and with more fatal results, for he has been trained to protect himself, to resist, to conquer....

Whatever may be said of man's protecting power in ordinary conditions, mid all the terrible disasters by land and sea, in the supreme moments of danger, alone woman must ever meet the horrors of the situation; the Angel of Death even makes no royal pathway for her. Man's love and sympathy enter only into the sunshine of our lives. In that solemn solitude of self, that links us with the immeasurable and the eternal, each soul lives alone forever....

Such is individual life. Who, I ask you, can take, dare take, on himself the rights, the duties, the responsibilities of another human soul?

To guide our own craft, we must be captain, pilot, engineer; with chart and compass to stand at the wheel...

Elizabeth Cady Stanton

Mary Church Terrell

Civil Rights Activist and Suffragist

When Mary Church Terrell delivered her poignant speech, 'What it Means to be Colored in the Capital of the United States', before a women's club in Washington, D.C., in 1906, she drew attention to the gap between American ideals of freedom and liberty and the harsh realities of Jim Crow laws. As an African-American woman in 1906, Terrell could not eat in the same restaurants, ride in the same car or stay in the same hotels as the white citizens of her city. 'As a colored woman I might enter Washington any night, a stranger in a strange land, and walk miles without finding a place to lay my head,' she told her audience.

At the time of her speech, Terrell had lived in Washington for over a decade, working as a language teacher and rising to a position on the District of Columbia Board of Education. Highly educated – she obtained a master's degree from Oberlin College, Ohio, in 1888 – she dazzled audiences abroad by delivering her lectures in English, German and French. In 1896, she was elected the first president of the newly formed National Association of Colored Women (NACW). Yet she remained dogged by deep-seated racism: 'It matters not what my intellectual attainments may be or how great is the need of the services of a competent person, if I try to enter many of the numerous vocations in which my white sisters are allowed to engage, the door is shut in my face.' In 1950, in her eighties, Terrell helped organize some of the first successful sit-ins to desegregate the capital's restaurants. She lived just long enough to see the United States Supreme Court declare the racial segregation of public schools unconstitutional in 1954.

... the chasm between the principles upon which this Government was founded ... and those which are daily practiced under the protection of the flag, yawns so wide and deep.

Mary Church Terrell

What It Means to be Colored in
the Capital of the United States 1906

Washington, D.C., has been called "The Colored Man's Paradise." Whether this sobriquet was given to the national capital in bitter irony by a member of the handicapped race, as he reviewed some of his own persecutions and rebuffs, or whether it was given immediately after the war by an ex-slaveholder who for the first time in his life saw colored people walking about like free men, minus the overseer and his whip, history saith not. It is certain that it would be difficult to find a worse misnomer for Washington than "The Colored Man's Paradise" if so prosaic a consideration as veracity is to determine the appropriateness of a name.

... As a colored woman I may walk from the Capitol to the White House, ravenously hungry and abundantly supplied with money with which to purchase a meal, without finding a single restaurant in which I would be permitted to take a morsel of food, if it was patronized by white people, unless I were willing to sit behind a screen. As a colored woman I cannot visit the tomb of the Father of this country, which owes its very existence to the love of freedom in the human heart and which stands for equal opportunity to all, without being forced to sit in the Jim Crow section of an electric car which starts from the very heart of the city – midway between the Capitol and the White House. If I refuse thus to be humiliated, I am cast into jail and forced to pay a fine for violating the Virginia laws. Every hour in the day Jim Crow cars filled with colored people, many of whom are intelligent and well to do, enter and leave the national capital.

... It is impossible for any white person in the United States, no matter how sympathetic and broad, to realize what life would mean to him if his incentive to effort were suddenly snatched away. To the lack of incentive to effort, which is the awful shadow under which we live, may be traced the wreck and ruin of scores of colored youth. And surely nowhere in the world do oppression and persecution based solely on the color of the skin appear more hateful and hideous than in the capital of the United States, because the chasm between the principles upon which this Government was founded, in which it still professes to believe, and those which are daily practiced under the protection of the flag, yawns so wide and deep.

Ida B. Wells
Journalist and Civil Rights Activist

Pioneering investigative journalist Ida B. Wells captivated a nation when she published a searing series of articles on the prevalence of mob violence and the lynching of black men in the United States. Born into slavery just before the end of the Civil War, Wells became a prominent writer and editor in Memphis, Tennessee, where she helped run a newspaper, the *Free Speech*. In the 1890s, after she penned an anti-lynching editorial in response to several high-profile murders, Wells's paper was destroyed by outraged readers and she fled the South. In New York, she published the pamphlet 'Southern Horrors: Lynch Law in All Its Phases', writing in the preface, 'Somebody must show that the Afro-American race is more sinned against than sinning, and it seems to have fallen upon me to do so.'

In a speech delivered at the National Negro Conference – an early African-American empowerment group – Wells presented her findings, addressing a myth often used to justify lynchings in the South: fears of miscegenation and sexual violence against white women. 'The lynching record for a quarter of a century merits the thoughtful study of the American people,' she began. 'It presents three salient facts: First, lynching is color-line murder. Second, crimes against women is the excuse, not the cause. Third, it is a national crime and requires a national remedy.' Wells helped found the National Association for the Advancement of Colored People in 1909, and remained a powerful advocate for African-Americans until her death in 1931.

This Awful Slaughter 1909

Why is mob murder permitted by a Christian nation? What is the cause of this awful slaughter? This question is answered almost daily—always the same shameless falsehood that "Negroes are lynched to protect womanhood." ... This is the never-varying answer of lynchers and their apologists. All know that it is untrue....

Is there a remedy, or will the nation confess that it cannot protect its protectors at home as well as abroad? Various remedies have been suggested to abolish the lynching infamy, but year after year, the butchery of men, women and children continues in spite of plea and protest....

The only certain remedy is an appeal to law. Lawbreakers must be made to know that human life is sacred ...

In a multitude of counsel there is wisdom. Upon the grave question presented by the slaughter of innocent men, women and children there should be an honest, courageous conference of patriotic, law-abiding citizens anxious to punish crime promptly, impartially and by due process of law, also to make life, liberty, and property secure against mob rule.

Time was when lynching appeared to be sectional, but now it is national—a blight upon our nation, mocking our laws and disgracing our Christianity. "With malice toward none but with charity for all" let us undertake the work of making the "law of the land" effective and supreme upon every foot of American soil—a shield to the innocent; and to the guilty punishment swift and sure.

Countess Markievicz
Suffragette and Politician

When the Irish revolutionary and suffragette Constance Markievicz, also known as Countess Markievicz, became the first woman elected to the British House of Commons in 1918, she was serving out a sentence in London's Holloway Prison for anti-British activities. It was not the first time she had been jailed: two years earlier, she had been sentenced to death for participation in the 1916 Easter Rising, but was subsequently given life imprisonment instead (because of her gender, she was told). Even if she had not been in prison (and she was later freed, as part of a general amnesty for the uprising's leaders), she would not have taken her seat as a Member of Parliament. As a member of the Irish political party Sinn Féin, she was committed to Irish independence and would not swear an oath to England's king. Instead, she and other Sinn Féin members established an alternative parliament in Dublin, setting the stage for the Irish Civil War and a decades-long reckoning with independence.

Long before this, in 1909, Markievicz delivered a lecture before the Student's National Literary Society in Dublin. She preached the ideals of nationhood and self-sacrifice, encouraging her listeners to buy Irish goods, support Irish education and, if necessary, defend Ireland physically. At a time when Irish women were not active in state affairs, Markievicz urged them to support their native land. A strong woman unafraid to use a revolver, Markievicz argued for a larger role for women in every sector of public life.

Women, Ideals and the Nation 1909

Ireland wants her girls to help her to build up her national life. Their fresh, clean views of life, their young energies, have been long too hidden away and kept separate in their different homes. Bring them out and organise them, and lo! you will find a great new army ready to help the national cause. The old idea that a woman can only serve her nation through her home is gone, so now is the time; on you the responsibility rests. No one can help you but yourselves alone; you must make the world look upon you as citizens first, as women after. For each one of you there is a niche waiting— your place in the nation. Try and find it. It may be as a leader, it may be as a humble follower—perhaps in a political party, perhaps in a party of your own—but it is there, and if you cannot find it for yourself, no one can find it for you.

... To sum up in a few words what I want the Young Ireland women to remember from me. Regard yourselves as Irish, believe in yourselves as Irish, as units of a nation distinct from England, your conqueror, and as determined to maintain your distinctiveness and gain your deliverance. Arm yourselves with weapons to fight your nation's cause. Arm your souls with noble and free ideas. Arm your minds with the histories and memories of your country and her martyrs, her language, and a knowledge of her arts, and her industries. And if in your day the call should come for your body to arm, do not shirk that either.

May this aspiration towards life and freedom among the women of Ireland bring forth a Joan of Arc to free our nation!

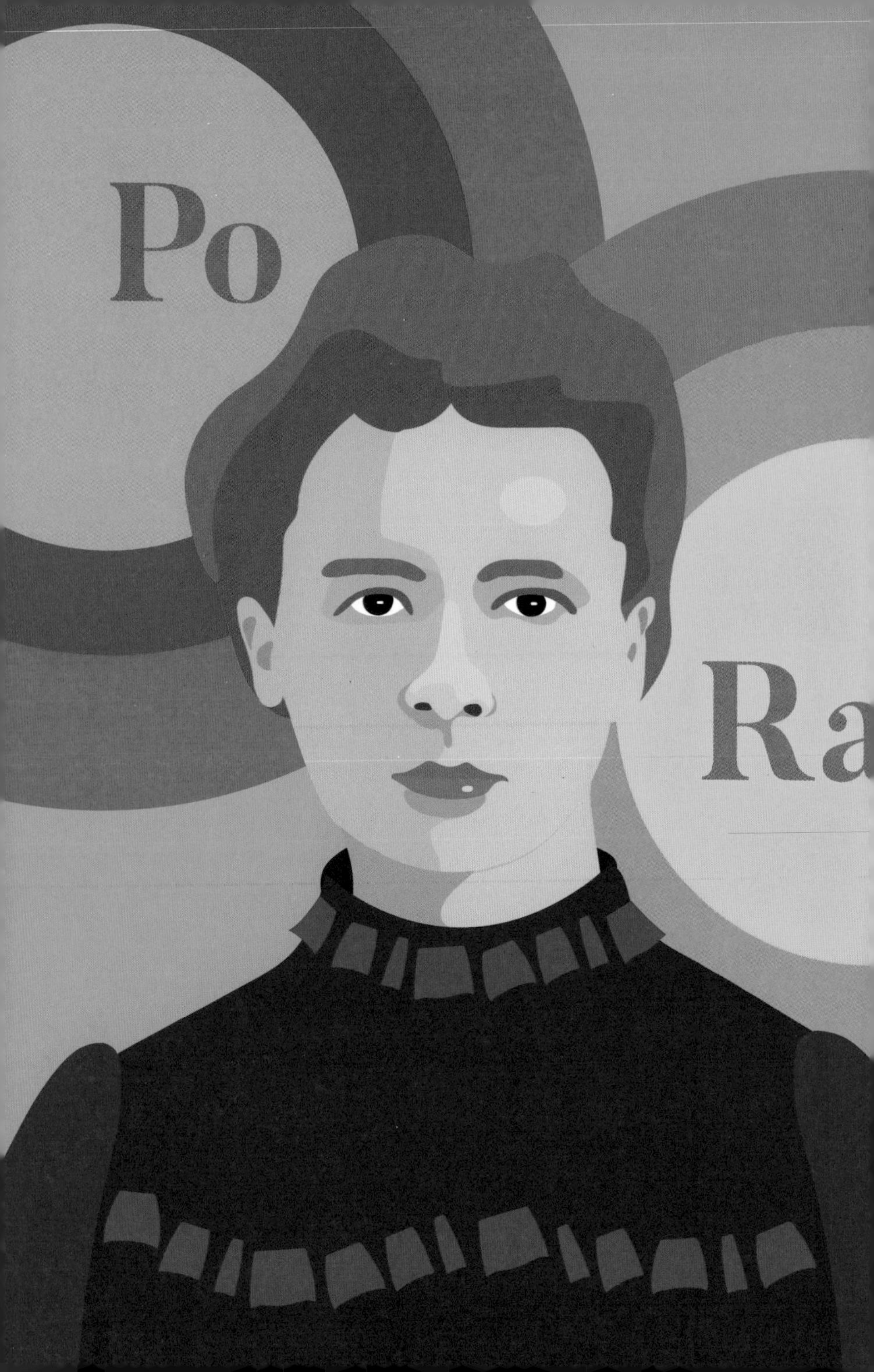
Po
Ra

Marie Curie
Physicist and Chemist

In 1911, when Marie Curie received the Nobel Prize in Chemistry, she became the world's first double Nobel laureate (to this day, just four people hold that distinction). When she travelled to Stockholm to accept the prize, she arrived on a wave of scandal and personal tragedy. Pierre Curie, her husband and lab partner, with whom she shared her first Nobel, in Physics, had died in a carriage accident five years earlier. Marie had since begun a new relationship with the married physicist Paul Langevin, and the French press would not leave her alone.

Marie's Nobel lecture describes the discovery of the elements radium and polonium, and outlines its implication for the new field of radioactivity. The speech was trailblazing in multiple ways. In 1903, when the Curies shared their award with Henri Becquerel, Pierre and Henri gave the lecture; as the first woman to win a Nobel, Marie was not asked to speak. Eight years later, accepting her solo award, she spoke alone, clearly defining her own work while acknowledging that the prize 'pays homage to the memory of Pierre Curie'.

Born in Poland, Marie spent most of her life in France, where she went on to found two institutes for the study of radioactivity and to use X-ray technology to aid wounded soldiers during the First World War. She taught for many years at the Sorbonne, where she was the first female lecturer and, in 1995, sixty years after her death, she became the first woman to be buried in Paris's famous Panthéon. Her daughter, Irène, won a shared Nobel in Chemistry with her husband, Frédéric Joliot, in 1935.

Nobel Lecture: Radium and the New Concepts in Chemistry 1911

Some 15 years ago the radiation of uranium was discovered by Henri Becquerel, and two years later the study of this phenomenon was extended to other substances, first by me, and then by Pierre Curie and myself. This study rapidly led us to the discovery of new elements, the radiation of which, while being analogous with that of uranium, was far more intense. All the elements emitting such radiation I have termed radioactive, and the new property of matter revealed in this emission has thus received the name radioactivity. Thanks to this discovery of new, very powerful radioactive substances, particularly radium, the study of radioactivity progressed with marvellous rapidity: Discoveries followed each other in rapid succession, and it was obvious that a new science was in course of development.

... Far from halting, the development of the new science has constantly continued to follow an upward course. And now, only 15 years after Becquerel's discovery, we are face to face with a whole world of new phenomena belonging to a field which, despite its close connexion with the fields of physics and chemistry, is particularly well-defined. In this field the importance of radium from the viewpoint of general theories has been decisive. The history of the discovery and the isolation of this substance has furnished proof of my hypothesis is that radioactivity is an atomic property of matter and can provide a means of seeking new elements. This hypothesis has led to present-day theories of radioactivity, according to which we can predict with certainty the existence of about 30 new elements which we cannot generally either isolate or characterize by chemical methods. We also assume that these elements undergo atomic transformations, and the most direct proof in favour of this theory is provided by the experimental fact of the formation of the chemically-defined element helium starting from the chemically-defined element radium.

Viewing the subject from this angle, it can be said that the task of isolating radium is the cornerstone of the edifice of the science of radioactivity. Moreover, radium remains the most useful and powerful tool in radioactivity laboratories. I believe that it is because of these considerations that the Swedish Academy of Sciences has done me the very great honour of awarding me this year's Nobel Prize for Chemistry.

It is therefore my task to present to you radium in particular as a new chemical element....

Discoveries followed each other in rapid succession, and it was obvious that a new science was in course of development.

Marie Curie

Emmeline Pankhurst
Suffragette

Emmeline Pankhurst's idea of a well-mannered lady was a woman who dressed meticulously, lived fashionably and embraced militant politics at all costs. Along with her daughter, Christabel, Pankhurst led the radical, female-only Women's Social and Political Union (WSPU), founded in 1903. Fed up with the polite tactics of other British suffrage groups, the WSPU pursued an uncompromising strategy. They began with marches and soapboxes, and soon moved into arson, bombs and acid. WSPU women broke windows, slashed paintings, chained themselves to railings and refused to pay taxes. One member, Emily Davison, famously died by throwing herself in front of the king's horse at the 1913 Epsom Derby.

By the time Pankhurst visited the United States in 1913 to raise funds for the WSPU, she had been jailed several times. The long speech she delivered to an audience of men and women at the Connecticut Women's Suffrage Association, then led by Katharine Houghton Hepburn (the Hollywood actress's mother), is both forthright and wryly self-aware. She describes the hunger strikes and force-feeding British suffragettes had endured. She points to the hypocrisy of a revolution that does not include women; wondering, for instance, why the Boston Tea Party men did not follow the tea dumping by also 'throwing the whiskey overboard'. She is pragmatic about violence ('you cannot make omelettes without breaking eggs'), and doggedly optimistic about the power of a women's movement. 'We wear no mark; we belong to every class,' she declares, 'The dear men of my country are discovering it is absolutely impossible to deal with it: you cannot locate it, and you cannot stop it.'

Freedom or Death 1913

*I am here as a soldier who has temporarily left the field of
battle in order to explain – it seems strange it should have to
be explained – what civil war is like when civil war is waged by
women.... I am here as a person who, according to the law
courts of my country, it has been decided, is of no value to the
community at all: and I am adjudged because of my life to be
a dangerous person, under sentence of penal servitude in a
convict prison.... I dare say, in the minds of many of you ... that
I do not look either very like a soldier or very like a convict,
and yet I am both.*

*... Now, I want to say to you who think women cannot
succeed, we have brought the government of England to this
position, that it has to face this alternative: either women are
to be killed or women are to have the vote. I ask American
men in this meeting, what would you say if in your state you
were faced with that alternative, that you must either kill
them or give them their citizenship...? Well, there is only one
answer to that alternative; there is only one way out ... you
must give those women the vote....*

*You won your freedom in America when you had the
revolution, by bloodshed, by sacrificing human life. You won
the civil war by the sacrifice of human life when you decided
to emancipate the negro. You have left it to women in your
land, the men of all civilised countries have left it to women, to
work out their own salvation. That is the way in which we
women of England are doing. Human life for us is sacred, but
we say if any life is to be sacrificed it shall be ours; we won't
do it ourselves, but we will put the enemy in the position
where they will have to choose between giving us freedom or
giving us death.*

*... So here am I. I come in the intervals of prison
appearance: I come after having been four times imprisoned
under the 'Cat and Mouse Act', probably going back to be
rearrested as soon as I set my foot on British soil. I come to
ask you to help to win this fight. If we win it, this hardest of all
fights, then, to be sure, in the future it is going to be made
easier for women all over the world to win their fight when
their time comes....*

If we win it, this hardest of all fights, then, to be sure, in the future it is going to be made easier for women all over the world to win their fight when their time comes.

Emmeline Pankhurst

Nellie McClung

Author and Suffragist

The day before Canadian author and suffragist Nellie McClung performed this spectacular act of satire at a theatrical 'Mock Parliament' in 1914, she attended a very similar speech made by Sir Rodmond Roblin, premier of the Manitoba province. At a Legislative Assembly meeting packed with women asking for the vote, Roblin argued against women's suffrage, naming, among other reasons, woman's sweet and maternal nature. McClung took careful mental notes. 'He never had a closer listener in all his life. I observed every gesture, the attitude he struck when he caught his thumbs in the armholes of his coat, twiddling his little fingers and teetering on his heels,' she later wrote in her autobiography. 'He was making the speech that I would make in the play in less than thirty-six hours. O, the delight of that moment!'

The following night, at a nearby theatre, McClung and other members of the Manitoba Political Equality League staged *A Woman's Parliament*, in which they held their own mock legislative meeting. In the alternative world of the play, women ruled the government and had come together to address a pressing question: Should men vote? McClung played the role of the premier, addressing the men and women in the audience with polite condescension, as she had seen Roblin do the previous day.

In 1916, Manitoba women became the first in Canada to win the right to vote. As McClung wrote in her 1921 novel *Purple Springs*, 'People seem to see a joke better sometimes when it is turned around'.

... Oh no, no, man was made for something higher and holier than voting.

Nellie McClung

Should Men Vote? 1914

Gentlemen of the Delegation:—

It gives me great pleasure to welcome you here to-day, – we like delegations, and altho this is the first time you have asked us for the vote, we hope it will not be the last.... We wish to congratulate you too, on the quiet, and ladylike way in which you have come into our presence ...

But I cannot do what you ask me to do, for the facts are all against you!...

Manhood suffrage would plunge our fair province into a perfect debauchery of extravagance, a perfect nightmare of expense.... You are asking me to put men, not only under clouds, but under barns, and I tell you frankly, I wont do it, for I have always loved and reverenced men.

... Oh no, no, man was made for something higher and holier than voting. Men were made to support families and homes which are the bulwark of the nation. What is home without a father? What is home without a bank account?... Shall I call men away from the useful plow and the necessary harrow to talk loud on street corners about things which do not concern them!...

In the United States of America when men vote, there is one divorce for every marriage, – for politics unsettle men, and that leads to unsettled bills, and broken furniture, and broken vows. When you ask me for the vote, you are asking me to break up peaceful and happy homes and wreck innocent lives, and I tell you again frankly, I will not do it. I am an old-fashioned woman, I believe in the sanctity of marriage.

... Men in politics have given us many unhappy examples – Nero, Herod, King John, are not worthy heroes, and yet you want me to hold up these men before our young people; I wonder any man ever dare ask for the vote in the light of such examples as these.

... With your little brain you cannot grasp what it means to run a Government such as this. Brains like yours only come in boys' sizes. But you think you can dictate to me, a woman who was busy running Governments when you were sitting in your high chair, drumming on a tin plate with a spoon!

... my most earnest wish for this bright land of Promise is that I may long be spared to guide its destiny among the nations of the earth.... [I must] go forward in the strong hope that I may long be spared to be the proud standard bearer of the grand old Flag of this grand old party, which has gone down many times to disgrace, but thank God! never defeat!

Jutta Bojsen-Møller

Chairwoman of the Danish Women's Society (1894–1910)

At the top of the Danish hill Himmelbjerget, where moments of national importance have been celebrated for over two centuries, stands a large oak tree. It was planted in 1915 to commemorate a new constitution that gave all Danish women, and previously disenfranchised men, the right to vote. At the age of seventy-eight, the Danish suffragette Jutta Bojsen-Møller had been working most of her adult life towards this achievement. In 1908, as Chairwoman of the Danish Women's Society, she helped secure voting rights for women in local elections. When the new constitution was finally ratified, expanding rights to the national vote, she cheered from the gallery in Parliament.

'Now, it is we women who are most appreciative of the new constitution; for the men, it is just an extension; for us, it is the whole thing,' Bojsen-Møller declared in a speech the following day, 6 June 1915. Using a poetic framework, she described the long struggle towards women's suffrage as similar to the progress made by hundreds of small trees, which slowly but steadily conquered an entire mountain, in a story by Norwegian writer Bjørnstjerne Bjørnson. Like the trees at the top, Bojsen-Møller suggests, enfranchised women can now look about themselves, taking stock of the world and assessing plans for the future.

Victory for Votes 1915

And so I have the pleasure of standing here on "Heaven's Hill" [Himmelbjerget], even in this life, and on the spot above this point I shall shortly have the honour of inaugurating a beautiful oak tree, which has been planted to commemorate yesterday - the day that afforded women equal rights with men. We cannot then but think of the Norwegian writer Bjørnstjerne Bjørnson's tale about the little trees that took it upon themselves to clothe the mountain. When finally, after much resistance - the worst being from the mountain itself - they reached the top, some of them exclaimed: "Well! Reaching one's destination certainly lifts the spirits."

And so too with us women today. We have also been fighting for half a century, in the face of great resistance, derision and taunting from the outset - worst of all from women themselves - and now we have finally reached our goal. Just like those small trees, we too may exclaim: "Well! Winning a victory certainly lifts the spirits."

... But now - now we rejoice. Now that ray of sunshine has reappeared, and with great force and clarity, now that women and domestic servants have been embraced; now we can indeed sing with truth: "Never will this day be forgotten". The day 5 June 1915 will be celebrated by the navelwort in the field and by Danish women alike.

... But now we have scaled the hill and are looking around like those small trees. And what, pray, do we see? The world ablaze with murder and horror. And indeed, like the German journalist Matthias Claudius in the Wandsbeck Messenger, we must say: "War! War! Good that I am not to blame for that". And yet, along with Bjørnson, we must also say: "For we let the country burn rather than have it go to wrack and ruin". But it would not have fallen into disarray, and now that we women have been given the right to vote and, like the men, will be blamed for everything that comes to pass in our fatherland, let us actively strive to find a different way of settling conflicts than by killing one another and burning the land.

Emma Goldman
Political Activist

When the anarchist Emma Goldman arrived in New York from Russia with her sister, Helena, in 1885, she swooned at the sight of the Statue of Liberty. 'Our spirits were high, our eyes filled with tears,' she later remembered. Goldman's patriotism for her adopted country took the form of a fiery activism. Magnetic and persuasive, she gave many lectures during her long life, rallying crowds around workers' rights, free speech, free love and birth control (she was a mentor to Margaret Sanger, see page 62).

In 1917, after President Woodrow Wilson initiated the draft for the First World War, Goldman and her collaborator, Alexander Berkman, helped found the No-Conscription League, an anti-war society. That same year, their offices were raided and they were charged and convicted of conspiring to obstruct the draft under the Espionage Act. Goldman was sentenced to two years in prison, after which she was deported to Russia. She was never again allowed to settle in the United States.

In her address to the jury, Goldman offers an impassioned defence of the 'conscientious objector'. 'Is he really a shirker, a slacker, or a coward?' she asked. 'Remember that those who fought and bled for your liberties were in their time considered as being against the law, as dangerous disturbers and trouble-makers.' She called the founding fathers 'the Anarchists of their time', and argued that new ideas are often outside the law: 'Progress knows nothing of fixity. It cannot be pressed into a definite mould.'

Address to the Jury 1917

May there not be different kinds of patriotism as there are different kinds of liberty? I for one cannot believe that love of one's country must needs consist in blindness to its social faults.... Neither can I believe that the mere accident of birth in a certain country or the mere scrap of a citizen's paper constitutes the love of country.

I know many people—I am one of them—who were not born here, and who yet love America with deeper passion and greater intensity than many natives whose patriotism manifests itself by pulling, kicking, and insulting those who do not rise when the national anthem is played. Our patriotism is that of the man who loves a woman with open eyes. He is enchanted by her beauty, yet he sees her faults. So we, too, who know America, love her beauty, her richness, her great possibilities... but with the same passionate emotion we hate her superficiality, her cant, her corruption....

We say that if America has entered the war to make the world safe for democracy, she must first make democracy safe in America. How else is the world to take America seriously, when democracy at home is daily being outraged, free speech suppressed.... We further say that a democracy conceived in the military servitude of the masses, in their economic enslavement... is not democracy at all. It is despotism—the cumulative result of a chain of abuses which, according to that dangerous document, the Declaration of Independence, the people have the right to overthrow.

Nancy Astor

First Female MP to Sit in the British House of Commons (1919–45)

For two years, Nancy Astor, a sharp-tongued American from Virginia, was the sole woman to serve as a Member of Parliament in the British House of Commons. Although she was not the first woman to be elected a Member of Parliament (that was Countess Markievicz; see page 42), she was the first to take her seat. Years later, she recalled her discomfort on 24 February 1920, making her maiden speech before her all-male colleagues (they would rather have greeted a rattlesnake, she said). Adding to her stress that day must have been the knowledge that her topic was in general deeply unpopular: temperance.

Yet Astor knew how to hold a room. After marrying Waldorf Astor, in 1906, she spent years entertaining at their grand estate, Cliveden, honing connections and becoming well-known for her wit. When her husband vacated the Commons in order to take his father's place in the House of Lords, Astor decided to make a bold run for his seat. She stayed in office for twenty-five years, championing social reform causes and recruiting women into government work (she considered herself a feminist). She was not always on the right side of history – she made some troubling anti-Catholic and anti-Semitic statements in her later years – but she created space for women in a place where previously there was none. As she told her audience in her maiden speech. 'I am simply trying to speak for hundreds of women and children throughout the country who cannot speak for themselves.'

Maiden Speech in Parliament 1920

I know that it was very difficult for some hon. Members to receive the first Lady M.P. into the House. It was almost as difficult for some of them as it was for the lady M.P. herself to come in. Hon. Members, however, should not be frightened of what Plymouth sends out into the world. After all, I suppose when Drake and Raleigh wanted to set out on their venturesome careers some cautious person said, "Do not do it; it has never been tried before. Stay at home, cruising in home waters." I have no doubt that the same thing occurred when the Pilgrim Fathers set out. I have no doubt that there were cautious Christian brethren who did not understand their going into the wide seas to worship God in their own way. But, on the whole, the world is all the better for those venturesome and courageous West Country people, and I would like to say that I am quite certain that the women of the whole world will not forget that it was the fighting men of Devon who dared to send the first woman to the Mother of Parliaments. It is only right that she should show some courage, and I am perfectly aware that it needs courage to address the House on that vexed question, Drink. However, I dare do it.

… I do not think the country is ripe for Prohibition, but I am certain it is ripe for drastic drink reforms. I know what I am talking about, and you must remember that women have got votes now and we mean to use them, and use them wisely, not for the benefit of any section, but for the benefit of the whole of society.

Margaret Sanger
Women's Rights Activist and Social Reformer

On the last day of the First American Birth Control Conference, held in New York City in November 1921, Margaret Sanger was arrested for disorderly conduct. She had planned to deliver the conference's closing speech before a public audience at Town Hall, but arrived to find the doors barricaded by policemen. Years later, she recalled wedging her way inside and beginning to speak, before being taken to police headquarters (she was released the following day). One week later, she finally delivered her speech, 'The Morality of Birth Control', at the Park Theatre, to a much larger audience, drawn in part by the controversy.

Nearly a century later, 'The Morality of Birth Control', which neatly summarized Sanger's views on contraception, remains polarizing. Sanger, who opened America's first birth control clinic in 1916, believed every child should be a wanted child. Every woman, she argued, should have the right to decide whether or not to give birth – and when, and how many times. While Sanger fought passionately for women's rights all her life, her legacy has come under fire in recent years. She has been criticized, like others of her time, for racist attitudes and a belief in eugenics. Nonetheless, she left an indelible imprint: in 1942, the American Birth Control League, which she founded, changed its name to the Planned Parenthood Federation of America. With an advocacy arm, and over 600 health centers across the United States, Planned Parenthood remains one of the strongest champions of women's reproductive rights.

The Morality of Birth Control 1921

We know that every advance that woman has made in the last half century has been made with opposition, all of which has been based upon the grounds of immorality.... When women asked for the franchise it was said that this would lower her standard of morals, that it was not fit that she should meet with and mix with the members of the opposite sex, but we notice that there was no objection to her meeting with the same members of the opposite sex when she went to church. The church has ever opposed the progress of woman on the ground that her freedom would lead to immorality. We ask the church to have more confidence in women. We ask the opponents of this movement to reverse the methods of the church, which aims to keep women moral by keeping them in fear and in ignorance... If we cannot trust woman with the knowledge of her own body, then I claim that two thousand years of Christian teaching has proved to be a failure.

We stand on the principle that Birth Control should be available to every adult man and woman. We believe that every adult man and woman should be taught the responsibility and the right use of knowledge. We claim that woman should have the right over her own body and to say if she shall or if she shall not be a mother, as she sees fit. We further claim that the first right of a child is to be desired. While the second right is that it should be conceived in love, and the third, that it should have a heritage of sound health.

Upon these principles the Birth Control movement in America stands.

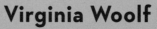

Virginia Woolf
Author and Journalist

In January 1931, Virginia Woolf addressed an audience from the Women's Service League, and a version of her speech was later published in the posthumous collection, *The Death of the Moth and Other Essays*. By the time she delivered 'Professions for Women', on the subject of work and women, the English author had already produced some of her best-known novels: *Mrs Dalloway*, *To The Lighthouse* and *Orlando*. She had also published *A Room of One's Own*, a landmark feminist essay in which she outlines, in lyrical language, the importance of an independent income for women. Woolf, who had a small inheritance, argued that financial independence allows the space and freedom for creative work.

In 'Professions for Women', Woolf examined the subtle ways in which women self-censor. She describes sitting down to write and bumping up against something hard: an ideal of Victorian womanhood, pervasive at the time, which she nicknames 'The Angel in the House'. In soothing tones, Woolf's 'Angel' advises her to flatter and to charm; to be gentle and self-sacrificing and to avoid, above all, telling the truth. Later, Woolf reflects on this inner struggle – a battle she had to win in order to write honestly. On the outside, she notes, there seem to be no obstacles which would make writing a book more difficult for a woman than for a man. But inside the mind, where phantoms like Woolf's 'Angel' lurk, it's a different story. A woman must overcome the prejudices she has internalized in order to find her voice, Woolf suggests.

Professions for Women 1931

What could be easier than to write articles and to buy Persian cats with the profits? But wait a moment. Articles have to be about something. Mine, I seem to remember, was about a novel by a famous man. And while I was writing this review, I discovered that if I were going to review books I should need to do battle with a certain phantom. And the phantom was a woman, and when I came to know her better I called her after the heroine of a famous poem, The Angel in the House. It was she who used to come between me and my paper when I was writing reviews. It was she who bothered me and wasted my time and so tormented me that at last I killed her. You who come of a younger and happier generation may not have heard of her—you may not know what I mean by the Angel in the House.

I will describe her as shortly as I can. She was intensely sympathetic. She was immensely charming. She was utterly unselfish. She excelled in the difficult arts of family life. She sacrificed herself daily. If there was chicken, she took the leg; if there was a draught she sat in it—in short she was so constituted that she never had a mind or a wish of her own, but preferred to sympathize always with the minds and wishes of others. Above all—I need not say it—she was pure. Her purity was supposed to be her chief beauty—her blushes, her great grace.... And when I came to write I encountered her with the very first words. The shadow of her wings fell on my page; I heard the rustling of her skirts in the room. Directly, that is to say, I took my pen in my hand to review that novel by a famous man, she slipped behind me and whispered: "My dear, you are a young woman. You are writing about a book that has been written by a man. Be sympathetic; be tender; flatter; deceive; use all the arts and wiles of our sex. Never let anybody guess that you have a mind of your own. Above all, be pure." And she made as if to guide my pen.... I turned upon her and caught her by the throat. I did my best to kill her. My excuse, if I were to be had up in a court of law, would be that I acted in self-defence. Had I not killed her she would have killed me. She would have plucked the heart out of my writing.

... I acted in self-defence. Had I not killed her she would have killed me. She would have plucked the heart out of my writing.

Virginia Woolf

Huda Sha'arawi
Women's Rights Activist

The Egyptian feminist Huda Sha'arawi spent her childhood among the women of her father's harem in Cairo, during the last years of a system steeped in tradition. Born into a wealthy, upper-class family in 1879, she wore a veil in public and entered into an arranged marriage with an older cousin at the age of thirteen. Always intellectually curious, she developed a sense of independence through an education with private tutors and by living away from her husband for seven years – unusual for the time. In 1919, when a nationalist movement broke out in Egypt, she played an active role, organizing anti-British demonstrations and serving as president of a nationalist women's committee. In 1923, the year after her husband died, Sha'arawi travelled to Rome to attend the International Alliance of Women Conference. On returning to Cairo, she stood at a train station before a group of women who had come to greet her, and slowly removed her veil. It was a radical act, performative and symbolic of a new era for Egypt's women.

In 1944, after years of activism, including the founding of the Egyptian Feminist Union, Sha'arawi spoke before a mixed audience at the first Arab Feminist Conference, in Cairo, which she had helped to organize. It was shortly before she helped found the Arab Feminist Union. In bold statements, Sha'arawi outlines the demands of Arab feminists and points towards a path forward for the movement. She argues that the *Sharia*, or Islamic law, grants women equal rights with men. If women are unequal, she suggests, it is only because men have abused their privileges. In clear, forthright language, she demands that society restore to women the rights she feels have been unjustly taken from them.

Speech at the Arab Feminist Conference 1944

Ladies and Gentlemen, the Arab woman who is equal to the man in duties and obligations will not accept, in the twentieth century, the distinctions between the sexes that the advanced countries have done away with. The Arab woman will not agree to be chained in slavery and to pay for the consequences of men's mistakes with respect to her country's rights and the future of her children. The woman also demands with her loudest voice to be restored her political rights, rights granted to her by the Sharia and dictated to her by the demands of the present. The advanced nations have recognised that the man and the woman are to each other like the brain and heart are to the body; if the balance between these two organs is upset the system of the whole body will be upset. Likewise, if the balance between the two sexes in the nation is upset it will disintegrate and collapse. The advanced nations ... have come to believe in the equality of sexes in all rights even though their religious and secular laws have not reached the level Islam has reached in terms of justice towards the woman.... The woman, given by the Creator the right to vote for the successor of the Prophet, is deprived of the right to vote for a deputy in a circuit or district election by a (male) being created by God. At the same time, this right is enjoyed by a man who might have less education and experience than the woman. And she is the mother who has given birth to the man and has raised him and guided him. The Sharia ... has made her equal to the man in all rights and responsibilities, even in the crimes that either sex can commit. However, the man who alone distributes rights, has kept for himself the right to legislate and rule, generously turning over to his partner his own share of responsibilities and sanctions without seeking her opinion about the division. The woman today demands to regain her share of rights that have been taken from her and gives back to the man the responsibilities and sanctions he has given to her. Gentlemen, this is justice, and I do not believe that the Arab man who demands that the others give him back his usurped rights would be avaricious and not give the woman back her own lawful rights, all the more so since he himself has tasted the bitterness of deprivation and usurped rights.

The woman also demands with her loudest voice to be restored her political rights, rights granted to her by the *Sharia* and dictated to her by the demands of the present.

Huda Sha'arawi

Funmilayo Ransome-Kuti
Political and Women's Rights Activist

In the mid-1940s, Funmilayo Ransome-Kuti emerged as one of the strongest voices for Nigerian women. In the aftermath of the Second World War, the financially strapped British colonial powers then occupying the country were imposing taxes on the market women of Nigeria. In the city of Abeokuta, in southwestern Nigeria, the women faced new quotas and random confiscations of their goods, enforced by the British-backed alake, or king of the town. Ransome-Kuti, then an instructor at Abeokuta Grammar School, was paying close attention. She began organizing the town's market women, many of whom were already her students and planned mass demonstrations – some saw close to 10,000 participants – under the banner of the Abeokuta Women's Union (AWU). In 1949, under mounting pressure, the alake abdicated and the tax on women was revised.

What began as a local effort soon became a national movement. The AWU was renamed the Nigerian Women's Union (NWU) in 1949, and chapters were founded in cities across the country, with membership reaching 20,000 women at its peak. A natural leader and an eloquent speaker, Ransome-Kuti travelled frequently to rouse groups of women into action. Often, she was working to develop chapters of the NWU. In 'A Talk About Women', likely from 1949, she speaks directly to the parents of girls, asking them to provide their daughters with the same education they would offer their sons. (Ransome-Kuti herself was the mother of three sons – including the Afrobeat artist Fela Kuti – and one daughter.) She went on to participate in the Nigerian independence movement, remaining a forceful advocate for woman until her death in 1978.

A Talk About Women c. 1949

How beautiful would it be if our women could have the same opportunity with men. A parent who had means to educate a child would rather educate his or her son, because he believed he would be receiving big salary when he had left school and took up a job..... The parent's poor daughters are neglected and left uneducated because the parent felt that whatever education she was given would be unprofitable and would all end in the kitchen. This sort of feeling which had existed for quite a long time was responsible for the state on women today. These poor girls eventually become relegated to the background, enslaved, enfeebled, uneducated, ignorant and absolutely silenced and suppressed in obscurity. They are overworked and underfed, yet they don't complain, because they are unconcious of their right. A wife is never a companion but a slave. As there is no country that can rise above her womenfolk, I am therefore appealing to the parents in this little article to give their daughters equal opportunity with their sons. I am also appealing to the men to please rally round and cooperate with women to redeem then from their present status. I am also saying to the women that "It is never too late to mend", "Rome was never built in a day". We women who are in the background today may be in the lime light tomorrow.

But the women too should strive to acquire knowledge in anything, from everywhere and anybody. They should try to take the best from all that comes their way.... There is such a lot of work before us, before we can take our place efficiently side by side with other women of the world, socially educationally, economically and so on, and pleased God, we shall.

Eva Perón

First Lady of Argentina (1946–52), Political Figure and Actress

By 1951, Eva Perón, better known as Evita, had transfixed a nation. Raised in poverty and abandoned by her father as a child, she built a successful radio and film career in Buenos Aires before marrying political hopeful Juan Perón, and soon after becoming the First Lady of Argentina.

During her husband's 1946 presidential campaign, Perón took an active role, using her platform to popularize his message and appearing – unusually for the time – by his side at rallies. In 1947, she travelled alone to represent Argentina on a goodwill tour of Europe and appeared on the cover of *Time* magazine. Perón also organized Argentina's first political party for women, the Female Perónist Party, which later proved decisive for her husband (Argentinian women gained the vote in 1947). Soon, her popularity rivalled that of Juan, and she seriously considered running as his vice-president.

However, other forces were at work. Perón was suffering from an aggressive form of cervical cancer, and by the time she spoke before a group of supporters – known affectionately as 'descamisados', or the shirtless – on 17 October 1951, she could hardly stand without assistance. In a passionate speech she played up the themes that had won her the admiration of the poorer classes of Argentina: selflessness, loyalty to her husband's vision and love for her people. 'My *descamisados*' she said. 'I have you in my hearts and tell you that it is certain my wish is that I will soon be back in the struggle, with more strength and love, to fight for this people which I love so much, as I love Perón.'

Speech to the *Descamisados* 1951

... What I say to Perón, who wanted to honor me with the highest distinction that could be granted a Perónist this evening, is that I will never cease repaying you and would give my life in gratitude for how good you have always been and are with me. Nothing I have, nothing I am, nothing I think is mine: it's Perón's. I will not tell you the usual lies: I won't tell you that I don't deserve this.... I deserve it for all I've done for the love of this people. I'm not important because of what I've done; I'm not important because of what I've renounced; I'm not important because of what I am or have. I have only one thing that matters, and I have it in my heart. It sets my soul aflame, it wounds my flesh and burns in my sinews: it's love for this people and for Perón.

... Compañeros, I ask just one thing today: that all of us publicly vow to defend Perón and to fight for him until death. And our oath will be shouted for a minute so that our cry can reach the last corner of the earth: Our lives for Perón!

Let the enemies of the people, of Perón and the Fatherland come. I have never been afraid of them because I have always believed in the people.... Though I leave shreds of my life along the road, I know that you will pick up my name and will carry it to victory as a banner. I know that God is with us because he is with the humble and despises the arrogance of the oligarchy. This is why victory will be ours. We will achieve it sooner or later, whatever the cost, whoever may fall.

Helen Keller

Political Activist and Author

Helen Keller's life changed dramatically when, at the age of nineteen months, she contracted an illness that left her both blind and deaf. Through extraordinary willpower, and the dedication of her longtime teacher and companion, Anne Sullivan, she was able to learn 'tactile fingerspelling' and, later, braille. In 1904, Keller graduated from Radcliffe College, a sister-college of Harvard University, becoming the first deafblind person to earn a Bachelor of Arts. Over the course of her long life (she lived well into her eighties), she was a passionate activist, travelling often to speak on behalf of the blind, as well as on socialism, pacifism and women's rights. A prolific author, she wrote a book of essays, *Out of the Dark*, detailing her views on socialism, as well as several books about her personal life, including her autobiography, *The Story of My Life*.

In 1952, Keller travelled to Paris to take part in centennial celebrations honouring Louis Braille. She was awarded a Medal of Chevalier of the Légion d'honneur and addressed an audience at the Sorbonne. She spoke in French, reaching the many Parisians who had come to hear her. 'Look at the strong solidarity that is already taking hold among blind people all over the world,' she said. 'This is truly a symbol of all the years in which blind people have broken through the darkness with the inner light of human knowledge.' In 1964, a few years before her death, she was awarded the Presidential Medal of Freedom, the United States' highest civilian honour.

The Life and Legacy of Louis Braille
1952

On behalf of the blind people of the world, I thank you from the bottom of my heart for having generously recognized the pride and efforts of all those who refuse to succumb to their limitations. In our way, we, the blind, are as indebted to Louis Braille as mankind is to Gutenberg. It is true that the dot system is very different from ordinary print, but these raised letters are, under our fingers, precious seeds from which has grown our intellectual harvest. Without the braille dot system, how incomplete and chaotic our education would be! The dismal doors of frustration would shut us out from the untold treasures of literature, philosophy and science. But, like a magic wand, the six dots of Louis Braille have resulted in schools where embossed books, like vessels, can transport us to ports of education, libraries and all the means of expression that assure our independence.

Look at the strong solidarity that is already taking hold among blind people all over the world, and how, thanks to international braille, they have begun to weave words of kinship among themselves and with humanity. This is truly a symbol of all the years in which blind people have broken through the darkness with the inner light of human knowledge. Blind people of the world simply ask that where their abilities have been successfully put to the test, they are given the chance to participate fully in the activities of their sighted counterparts.

Eleanor Roosevelt
First Lady of the United States (1933–45) and Diplomat

Eleanor Roosevelt's outspoken public career continued long after the death of her husband, the thirty-second president of the United States, Franklin D. Roosevelt. As first lady, Roosevelt redefined the terms of this role as an active and influential position of leadership. She spoke out publicly against racial discrimination and human rights violations, and she often gave speeches in her husband's place. In 1945, President Harry Truman appointed her a representative on the United States' first delegation to the United Nations General Assembly. Two years later, she was elected the first chair of the UN's newly formed Human Rights Commission, where she shepherded to completion a landmark document: the Universal Declaration of Human Rights.

Introducing the Declaration before the UN in 1948, Roosevelt said that she hoped it might come to be seen as a guiding source of moral authority. In many ways her hopes have been borne out: the Declaration has been translated into over 500 languages and has influenced the drafting of countless laws. In Roosevelt's time, however, it was still a hopeful and untested experiment, like the fledgling UN as a whole. In 1954, she addressed some of the public frustration with the UN before an audience at Brandeis University, in Massachusetts. At the height of McCarthyism and fears about the Soviet Union, Roosevelt reminded her listeners that progress is incremental and encouraged them to think of the UN's General Assembly 'as a place where bridges are built between peoples'.

The United Nations as a Bridge 1954

We in the United States are an impatient people. We want to see results tomorrow. I am not sure sometimes that it isn't the people who can outwait the other people, who have the advantage. Frequently, moving too fast can set you back.

People are meeting in the United Nations that come from backgrounds where there have been certain customs and habits for generations…. We might think occasionally that other people find their way the best, and not our way. There are things we can learn from other people. You must have as a basis to all understanding, the willingness to learn and the willingness to listen.

… When we look upon the failures in the United Nations, we should not be disheartened, because if we take the failure and learn, eventually we will use this machinery better…. No machinery works unless people make it work.

In a democracy like ours, it is the people who have to tell their representatives what they want them to do. And it is the acceptance of individual responsibility by each one of us that actually will make the United Nations machinery work. If we don't accept that, and if we don't do the job, we may well fail—but it lies in our hands….

We are the strongest nation in the world…. We lead not only in military and economic strength, but we lead in knowing what are our values, what are the things we believe in, and in being willing to live up to them, and being willing to accept the fact that living up to them here, we help ourselves, but we also help the world.

Shirley Chisholm
Member of the United States Congress
(1969–83)

When Shirley Chisholm made a passionate argument for the Equal Rights Amendment (ERA) in 1969, she did so as the first black woman to be elected to the United States Congress. First proposed in 1921, and still languishing today, proponents of the ERA sought an amendment that would guarantee equal rights under the law for all American citizens, regardless of sex. This included marriage and divorce laws, as well as workplace protections. In the late 1960s, with the endorsement of the newly formed National Organization for Women (NOW), momentum for passage of the ERA picked up again, and Chisholm helped lead the charge.

In crystal-clear language, Chisholm outlined for the US House of Representatives the prejudices that hold women back in the workplace. The child of Caribbean immigrants, she drew a connection between sexism and stereotypes and discrimination based on race. Her sense of injustice, as she recounts the statistics, is palpable: 'Women occupy only two percent of the managerial positions. They have not even reached the level of tokenism yet.' No women then sat on the Supreme Court, she reminded her audience, and women numbered just one senator and ten representatives in Congress. 'Considering that there are about 3.5 million more women in the United States than men, this situation is outrageous,' she said.

Chisholm's long career saw her serve in the House, as a representative from New York, until 1983. In 1972, she became the first black person, and the first woman, to seek the Democratic presidential nomination. Her Congressional campaign slogan was apt: 'Unbought and Unbossed'.

Equal Rights for Women 1969

Mr. Speaker, when a young woman graduates from college and starts looking for a job, she is likely to have a frustrating and even demeaning experience ahead of her. If she walks into an office for an interview, the first question she will be asked is, 'Do you type?'

There is a calculated system of prejudice that lies unspoken behind that question. Why is it acceptable for women to be secretaries, librarians, and teachers, but totally unacceptable for them to be managers, administrators, doctors, lawyers, and Members of Congress.

The unspoken assumption is that women are different. They do not have executive ability, orderly minds, stability, leadership skills, and they are too emotional.

It has been observed before, that society for a long time, discriminated against another minority, the blacks, on the same basis – that they were different and inferior....

As a black person, I am no stranger to race prejudice. But the truth is that in the political world I have been far oftener discriminated against because I am a woman than because I am black.

... laws will not change such deep-seated problems overnight. But they can be used to provide protection for those who are most abused, and to begin the process of evolutionary change by compelling the insensitive majority to reexamine its unconscious attitudes.

It is for this reason that I wish to introduce today a proposal that has been before every Congress for the last 40 years and that sooner or later must become part of the basic law of the land – the equal rights amendment.

... It is obvious that discrimination exists. Women do not have the opportunities that men do. And women that do not conform to the system, who try to break with the accepted patterns, are stigmatized as 'odd' and 'unfeminine'. The fact is that a woman who aspires to be chairman of the board, or a Member of the House, does so for exactly the same reasons as any man. Basically, these are that she thinks she can do the job and she wants to try.

... What we need are laws to protect working people, to guarantee them fair pay, safe working conditions, protection against sickness and layoffs, and provision for dignified, comfortable retirement. Men and women need these things equally. That one sex needs protection more than the other is a male supremacist myth as ridiculous and unworthy of respect as the white supremacist myths that society is trying to cure itself of at this time.

... women that do not
conform to the system,
who try to break with
the accepted patterns,
are stigmatized as 'odd'
and 'unfeminine'.

Shirley Chisholm

Ruth Bader Ginsburg
Supreme Court Justice (1993–2020)

When Ruth Bader Ginsburg entered Harvard Law School in 1956, she was one of just nine women in a class of around 500 men. Years later, as a professor at Rutgers Law School, in 1970, Ginsburg taught one of the country's first courses on women and the law (she had scant scholarship to draw from). Around the same time, she began an organized effort to argue on behalf of cases that she believed would work towards eliminating sex discrimination in public life. Her goal was to persuade the court to recognize sex, like race, as a 'suspect classification' – that is, a distinction that requires a standard of 'strict scrutiny' to uphold.

In 1973, Ginsburg took on *Frontiero v. Richardson*, a case in which Sharron Frontiero, a married air force officer, could not secure the same benefits for her dependent husband as those available for the dependent wives of male officers. In her stirring oral argument before the Supreme Court, Ginsburg outlined the ways in which sex-based laws undermine women, reaching back in time to quote from the abolitionist Sarah Grimké, Angelina's sister (see page 20). The court agreed, ruling in Frontiero's favour. 'There can be no doubt that our Nation has had a long and unfortunate history of sex discrimination,' Justice William Brennan wrote in the decision. 'Traditionally, such discrimination was rationalized by an attitude of "romantic paternalism" which, in practical effect, put women not on a pedestal, but in a cage.'

Ginsburg died on 18 September 2020

Argument in *Frontiero* v. *Richardson*
1973

Sex like race is a visible, immutable characteristic bearing no necessary relationship to ability.

… Women today face discrimination in employment as pervasive and more subtle than discrimination encountered by minority groups.

In vocational and higher education, women continue to face restrictive quotas no longer operative with respect to other population groups.

Their absence is conspicuous in Federal and State Legislative, Executive, and Judicial Chambers in higher civil service positions and in appointed posts in federal, state, and local government.

… Sex classifications do stigmatize when as in Goesaert against Cleary 235 U.S., they exclude women from an occupation thought more appropriate to men.

The sex criterion stigmatizes when it is used to limit hours of work for women only.

… The sex criterion stigmatizes when … it assumes that all women are preoccupied with home and children and therefore should be spared the basic civic responsibility of serving on a jury.

These distinctions have a common effect. They help keep woman in her place, a place inferior to that occupied by men in our society.

… In asking the Court to declare sex a suspect criterion, amicus urges a position forcibly stated in 1837 by Sarah Grimké … She said, "I ask no favor for my sex. All I ask of our brethren is that they take their feet off our necks."

Sylvia Rivera
LGBTQ Activist

In 1973, when the LGBTQ activist Sylvia Rivera jumped onstage and commandeered the microphone during the Christopher Street Liberation Day Rally in New York City, she was speaking up for a marginalized group within a marginalized group: the transgender community.

Orphaned at a young age, Rivera spent a rough adolescence on the street, where she developed a drag queen persona, and often turned to sex work. In 1970, she and her friend Marsha P. Johnson co-founded the organization Street Transvestite Action Revolutionaries (STAR), which provided shelter and support for homeless queer youth. Often, they catered to teenagers and runaways in need of a place to stay.

As an American of Puerto Rican and Venezuelan descent, Rivera frequently found herself at the nexus of multiple prejudices based on race, sexuality and gender nonconformity. These biases hampered her within the LGBTQ community as well, which at first did not see transgender concerns as a priority. While she was an active participant in the Stonewall riots, and an early member of both the Gay Liberation Front and the Gay Activists Alliance, she had to fight tooth and nail to make herself heard. In her 1973 speech, given at a precursor to New York City's Gay Pride Parade, her righteous fury at being denied a chance to speak is on full display – as is her charisma. Met at first by boos and jeers from the audience, she gradually wins them over until at last they are cheering with her: 'GAY POWER!'

Y'all Better Quiet Down 1973

Y'all better quiet down. I've been trying to get up here all day for your gay brothers and your gay sisters in jail....

Have you ever been beaten up and raped and jailed? Now think about it. They've been beaten up and raped.... The women have tried to fight for their sex changes or to become women.... they do not write women, they do not write men, they write 'STAR' because we're trying to do something for them.

I have been to jail. I have been raped. And beaten. Many times! By men, heterosexual men that do not belong in the homosexual shelter. But do you do anything for me? No. You tell me to go and hide my tail between my legs. I will not put up with this shit. I have been beaten. I have had my nose broken. I have been thrown in jail. I have lost my job. I have lost my apartment for gay liberation and you all treat me this way? What the fuck's wrong with you all? Think about that!

... I believe in the gay power. I believe in us getting our rights, or else I would not be out there fighting for our rights. That's all I wanted to say to you people ... come and see the people at Star House....

The people are trying to do something for all of us, and not men and women that belong to a white middle class white club. And that's what you all belong to! REVOLUTION NOW! Gimme a 'G'! Gimme an 'A'! Gimme a 'Y'! Gimme a 'P'! Gimme an 'O'! Gimme a 'W'! Gimme an 'E! Gimme an 'R'! Gay power! Louder! GAY POWER!

Simone Veil
French Minister of Health (1974–79)

In 1944, sixteen-year-old Simone Jacob was deported, along
with her mother and sisters, to the Auschwitz-Birkenau
concentration camp in occupied Poland. Born into a French-
Jewish family in Nice, France, she had just finished her
baccalaureate studies. Her father, brother and mother did not
survive the war, but Simone and her sisters did. After her
return to France, she excelled as a law student in Paris, and
soon married Antoine Veil, a civil servant. In 1974, she took up
the post of Minister of Health, championing women's rights,
including increased access to contraception. Five years later,
she became the first woman to be elected President of the
European Parliament.

In all of Veil's extraordinary career, she is best
remembered for her successful effort to legalize abortion in
France. Before 1975, the practice was illegal and highly
stigmatized (one of the last women to be guillotined in the
country was Marie-Louise Giraud, a struggling mother during
the Vichy regime, who performed at least twenty-seven
abortions before 1943). In the French Parliament, in 1974,
before a room filled almost entirely with men, Veil explained
the reasoning behind a bill which would legalize abortion for
women in the first ten weeks of pregnancy (later expanded to
twelve). She framed the debate in careful terms, suggesting
that the new law – the 'Veil law', as it came to be known –
would only be making safer procedures which were already
taking place. At the time of her death in 2017, at the age of
eighty-nine, she had established herself as one of France's
most widely admired public figures. In 2018, in a grand public
ceremony, she was buried in the Panthéon, in Paris, alongside
seventy-two of France's best-loved men and just four women,
including Marie Curie (see page 44).

... I say we are in a situation of chaos and anarchy that cannot go on.

Simone Veil

Speech to Parliament on Abortion Law 1974

Mr President, ladies, gentlemen; if I stand here today before this parliament, as health minister, as a woman and as a non-parliamentarian, to propose to the elected members of this country a profound change to the legislation on abortion, then believe me that it is with a deep sense of humility – facing both the difficulties of the problem itself, and indeed the strength of the very personal feelings that this subject evokes in every French man and woman, as well as being fully aware of the weight of responsibility that we are going to take on together.

But it is also with the strongest possible conviction that I will defend a project [which aims] to bring about a considered and human solution to one of the most difficult problems of our time.

... We have come to a point where, on this matter, the public authorities can no longer shirk their responsibilities. All the facts support this: the studies and work over the past several years, the commission hearings, the experiences of other European countries. And most of you can sense it – knowing that we can no longer stop illegal abortions, and yet nor can we apply criminal law against all the women who would be punishable by its rules.

... I say we are in a situation of chaos and anarchy that cannot go on.

... I say most sincerely: abortion must remain the exception, the last resort in a hopeless situation. But how can we condone abortion without it losing this special status, without society appearing to encourage it?

I would like first of all to share with you a belief held by all women – and I am sorry to do so before an Assembly almost exclusively made up of men: any woman seeking an abortion does so with a heavy heart. You just have to listen to the women....

... Currently, who looks after those women who find themselves in this situation? The law sends them away not only in disgrace, shame and isolation, but also into the anonymity and anxiety of legal proceedings. Forced to hide their pregnancy, all too often they find nobody to listen to them, advise them and give them support and protection.

Among those who today are fighting against any eventual modification of this punitive law, how many of those are concerned with helping these women in their distress? How many of those can think beyond what they might see as an offence, and have learned to show young single mothers the understanding and moral support that they really need?

Indira Gandhi
Prime Minister of India (1966–77; 1980–84)

Indira Gandhi served four terms as India's first female prime minister, beginning with her election in 1966 and ending with her assassination in 1984. The daughter of Jawaharlal Nehru, India's first prime minister, Gandhi was born into a life of politics. Her aggressive war policy and her centralization of power (she ruled by decree during a 'State of Emergency' from 1975 to 1977) left a complicated legacy. In 1980, she addressed an audience at a new building complex designed for the All-India Women's Conference, a women's empowerment group, in New Delhi. 'I have often said that I am not a feminist,' she began, 'Yet, in my concern for the underprivileged, how can I ignore women who, since the beginning of history, have been dominated over and discriminated against in social customs and in laws?'

Although Gandhi publically distanced herself from the term 'feminist', her position as the leader of the world's largest democracy made her, for many, a symbol of women's potential. In a deeply patriarchal society, she seemed to transcend gender. Perhaps out of fear of appearing weak, she mostly avoided speaking about her sex, and is often called 'The Iron Lady of India'. In appearing before the AIWC, however, she was paying tribute to a rich history of activism among women in India. Early on, these women-led organizations fought for educational opportunities, an end to child marriages and fairer divorce laws, among other issues. In her speech, Gandhi reflected that, 'by excluding women, men are depriving themselves of a fuller emancipation or growth for themselves.'

True Liberation of Women 1980

In the West, women's so-called freedom is often equated with imitation of man. Frankly, I feel that is merely an exchange of one kind of bondage for another. To be liberated, woman must feel free to be herself, not in rivalry to man but in the context of her own capacity and her personality. We need women to be more interested, more alive and more active not because they are women but because they do comprise half the human race.... Indian women are traditionally conservative but they also have the genius of synthesis, to adapt and to absorb. That is what gives them resilience to face suffering and to meet upheavals with a degree of calm, to change constantly and yet remain changeless, which is the quality of India herself.

Today's major concerns are: first, economic and social inequality and injustice.... Secondly, the anxiety whether human wisdom will prevail over what can only be called a death wish in which the desire to dominate expresses itself in countless ways, the most dangerous being the armament race. And, thirdly, the need to protect this, our only Earth, from human rapacity and exploitation....

These enormous challenges cannot be met only by some sections, however advanced they may be, while others pull in different directions or watch apathetically. The effort has to be a universal one, conscious and concerted, considering no one too small to contribute. The effort must embrace all nationalities and all classes regardless of religion, caste or sex.

Margaret Thatcher
Prime Minister of Great Britain (1979–90)

Ever controversial, Margaret Thatcher remains the longest serving prime minister in the UK's history, and has the distinction of being the first woman to hold the post. In her eleven years in office, she promoted the tenets of what came to be known as Thatcherism: deregulation, small government and free markets. She earned (and took pride in) the nickname 'The Iron Lady' for her tough stance towards Soviet Russia. However, critics accused her of championing harsh policies that produced a high unemployment rate. Throughout her long career in a sector dominated by men, she consistently let unkind remarks (many of them gendered) roll off her back, leaving her poised and unruffled.

During Thatcher's rise to leader of the Conservative party, she began taking speech lessons. Like many female politicians, she faced intense scrutiny over her voice, which the press had deemed 'shrill'. She wanted to move towards a lower, more commanding tone. In 1980, she gave a speech at the Conservative Party Conference in Brighton, in which her vocal prowess was on full display. In a clear and steady voice, she distilled her party's vision, using a dry wit to charm the room. (When a heckler interrupts, she pauses, and says, 'Never mind, it is wet outside. I expect that they wanted to come in. You cannot blame them; it is always better where the Tories are.') Towards the end, making reference to expectations that she would reverse some of her controversial economic policies, she delivers the famous line: 'You turn if you want to. The lady's not for turning.'

The Lady's Not for Turning 1980

Decent people do want to do a proper job at work, not to be restrained or intimidated from giving value for money. They believe that honesty should be respected, not derided. They see crime and violence as a threat not just to society but to their own orderly way of life. They want to be allowed to bring up their children in these beliefs, without the fear that their efforts will be daily frustrated in the name of progress or free expression.

... People yearn to be able to rely on some generally accepted standards. Without them you have not got a society at all, you have purposeless anarchy.... A great nation is the voluntary creation of its people—a people composed of men and women whose pride in themselves is founded on the knowledge of what they can give to a community of which they in turn can be proud.

If our people feel that they are part of a great nation and they are prepared to will the means to keep it great, a great nation we shall be, and shall remain. So, what can stop us from achieving this? What then stands in our way? The prospect of another winter of discontent? I suppose it might.

But I prefer to believe that certain lessons have been learnt from experience, that we are coming, slowly, painfully, to an autumn of understanding. And I hope that it will be followed by a winter of common sense....

To those waiting with bated breath for that favourite media catchphrase, the "U" turn, I have only one thing to say. "You turn if you want to. The lady's not for turning."

Ursula K. Le Guin
Novelist

When the novelist Ursula K. Le Guin delivered 'A Left-Handed Commencement Address' to the all-female graduates of Mills College, in the Bay Area, in 1983, she did so in what she called 'the language of women'. She began by acknowledging that commencements often assume a male audience. She noted dryly that graduation gowns, originally designed for men, make women look like either a 'mushroom or a pregnant stork'. 'Intellectual tradition is male. Public speaking is done in the public tongue, the national or tribal language; and the language of our tribe is men's language,' she said.

Le Guin – whose famous 1969 sci-fi novel, *The Left Hand of Darkness*, takes place on a planet populated by individuals without a fixed gender – did not want to communicate on those terms. She did not want to discuss success ('Success is somebody else's failure') or power, which she saw as belonging to a male tradition. She wishes the graduates children, if they want them, and turns her talk towards a radical rejection of patriarchal society (dubbed 'Machoman'). Le Guin encourages her audience to embrace failure, and to live as natives in a country of women. She muses: 'Instead of talking about power, what if I talked like a woman right here in public?'

What hope we have
lies there.... Not in the light
that blinds, but in the dark
that nourishes, where human
beings grow human souls.

———————————

Ursula K. Le Guin

A Left-Handed Commencement Address 1983

Because you are human beings you are going to meet failure. You are going to meet disappointment, injustice, betrayal, and irreparable loss. You will find you're weak where you thought yourself strong. You'll work for possessions and then find they possess you. You will find yourself - as I know you already have - in dark places, alone, and afraid.

What I hope for you, for all my sisters and daughters, brothers and sons, is that you will be able to live there, in the dark place. To live in the place that our rationalizing culture of success denies, calling it a place of exile, uninhabitable, foreign.

Well, we're already foreigners. Women as women are largely excluded from, alien to, the self-declared male norms of this society, where human beings are called Man, the only respectable god is male, the only direction is up. So that's their country; let's explore our own....

In our society, women have lived, and have been despised for living, the whole side of life that includes and takes responsibility for helplessness, weakness, and illness, for the irrational and the irreparable, for all that is obscure, passive, uncontrolled, animal, unclean - the valley of the shadow, the deep, the depths of life.... Well so that is our country. The night side of our country. If there is a day side to it ... we haven't got there yet. We're never going to get there by imitating Machoman. We are only going to get there by going our own way, by living there, by living through the night in our own country.

So what I hope for you is that you live there not as prisoners, ashamed of being women, consenting captives of a psychopathic social system, but as natives. That you will be at home there, keep house there, be your own mistress, with a room of your own. That you will do your work there, whatever you're good at.... And when you fail, and are defeated, and in pain, and in the dark, then I hope you will remember that darkness is your country, where you live, where no wars are fought and no wars are won, but where the future is. Our roots are in the dark; the earth is our country. Why did we look up for blessing - instead of around, and down? What hope we have lies there.... Not in the light that blinds, but in the dark that nourishes, where human beings grow human souls.

Barbara McClintock
Scientist and Cytogeneticist

When the ground-breaking geneticist Barbara McClintock won the Nobel Prize in Physiology or Medicine in 1983, she was being recognized for discoveries made decades earlier. In the late 1940s, she began experimenting with the maize plant, observing how hereditary characteristics, like the colour patterns of kernels on an ear of corn, for instance, changed over successive generations. In the 1940s and 1950s, the Nobel Committee explained, her research 'proved that genetic elements can sometimes change position on a chromosome and that this causes nearby genes to become active or inactive'. Genetic transposition, as this process is called today, has broad implications for evolutionary studies and disease control.

McClintock, who was born in Connecticut in 1902 and received her PhD from Cornell University in 1927, made many of her most important discoveries in obscurity. Some historians have suggested she was overlooked, or not taken seriously, because of her gender. In 1953, feeling isolated from the scientific community, she stopped publishing her research. Still, she continued her work, believing it would eventually be acknowledged ('One must await the right time for conceptual change,' she wrote many years later.) At the Nobel Prize ceremony, she gave a short, surprising banquet speech, in which she described her years working without recognition as 'a delight', for the uninterrupted freedom they provided.

Nobel Lecture 1983

Your Majesties, Your Royal Highnesses, Ladies and Gentlemen,

I am delighted to be here, and charmed by the warmth of the Swedish people. And I wish to thank them for their many courtesies.

I understand I am here this evening because the maize plant, with which I have worked for many years, revealed a genetic phenomenon that was totally at odds with the dogma of the times, the mid-nineteen forties. Recently, with the general acceptance of this phenomenon, I have been asked, notably by young investigators, just how I felt during the long period when my work was ignored, dismissed, or aroused frustration. At first, I must admit, I was surprised and then puzzled, as I thought the evidence and the logic sustaining my interpretation of it, were sufficiently revealing. It soon became clear, however, that tacit assumptions - the substance of dogma - served as a barrier to effective communication. My understanding of the phenomenon responsible for rapid changes in gene action, including variegated expressions commonly seen in both plants and animals, was much too radical for the time. A person would need to have my experiences, or ones similar to them, to penetrate this barrier. Subsequently, several maize geneticists did recognize and explore the nature of this phenomenon, and they must have felt the same exclusions. New techniques made it possible to realize that the phenomenon was universal, but this was many years later. In the interim I was not invited to give lectures or seminars, except on rare occasions, or to serve on committees or panels, or to perform other scientists' duties. Instead of causing personal difficulties, this long interval proved to be a delight. It allowed complete freedom to continue investigations without interruption, and for the pure joy they provided.

Corazon C. Aquino
President of the Philippines (1986–92)

In September 1986, Corazon Aquino gave a speech before the United States Congress. She had been President of the Philippines for just over half of a tumultuous year and was struggling to rebuild democratic processes abolished by the authoritarian regime of her predecessor, Ferdinand Marcos. Aquino's path to power was not straightforward. Her husband, Benigno Aquino Jr., had been one of Marcos's chief political rivals and, during Marcos's tenure, he was imprisoned, then exiled, and finally, in 1983, assassinated.

When Marcos called a snap election in 1985, Aquino, now a widow, was pressed by a 'one-million signature campaign' to run for the presidency. Marcos's government declared that he had won, but widespread fraud was suspected. People gathered on the streets for four days to demonstrate against the dictator. Marcos fled the country and Aquino took office by popular demand, becoming the Philippines's first female president.

One of her first acts was drafting a new constitution which enshrined democratic principles. In her speech before Congress, Aquino describes her country's commitment to the ideals of democracy, recalling voters undaunted by armed guards at the polls. Aquino styled herself as a reluctant leader thrust into politics by a sense of duty. However, by the time of her 1986 speech, she had become a powerful symbol of democracy in the Philippines. During her time in office, she struggled to unite a fractured country and revive a struggling economy. She stepped down in 1992. Her memory was revived in 2010 when her son was elected president, a year after her death. She was mourned by thousands as the 'Mother of Philippine Democracy'.

Speech During the Joint Session of the US Congress 1986

Last year, in an excess of arrogance, the dictatorship called for its doom in a snap election. The people obliged. With over a million signatures, they drafted me to challenge the dictatorship. And I obliged them. The rest is the history that dramatically unfolded on your television screen and across the front pages of your newspapers.

You saw a nation, armed with courage and integrity, stand fast by democracy against threats and corruption. You saw women poll watchers break out in tears as armed goons crashed the polling places to steal the ballots but, just the same, they tied themselves to the ballot boxes. You saw a people so committed to the ways of democracy that they were prepared to give their lives for its pale imitation. At the end of the day, before another wave of fraud could distort the results, I announced the people's victory.

... When a subservient parliament announced my opponent's victory, the people turned out in the streets and proclaimed me President. And true to their word, when a handful of military leaders declared themselves against the dictatorship, the people rallied to their protection. Surely, the people take care of their own. It is on that faith and the obligation it entails, that I assumed the presidency.

As I came to power peacefully, so shall I keep it. That is my contract with my people and my commitment to God.

... We have swept away absolute power by a limited revolution that respected the life and freedom of every Filipino.... So within about a year from a peaceful but national upheaval that overturned a dictatorship, we shall have returned to full constitutional government. Given the polarization and breakdown we inherited, this is no small achievement.

Naomi Wolf
Author

When American author Naomi Wolf published *The Beauty Myth* in 1991, she set off a national debate about unrealistic beauty standards and their harmful effects on women. Though the book was generally well-received, Wolf was criticized by news anchors, cosmetic surgeons and right-wing radio hosts who suggested there must be something wrong with her. Each time she was questioned, she recalled in a 1992 commencement speech at Scripps College, she would worry about offending her critics – about breaching unwritten rules of 'niceness' for women. Around that time, she read an essay by the poet and activist Audre Lorde, which argued that silence is not a form of protection, and Wolf began to change her approach. 'Today I want to give you a backlash survival kit,' she told the graduates.

In her speech, Wolf presents four 'messages' (message no. 1: 'redefine "becoming a woman"'). She points out that women are told they have 'become a woman' after biological events such as childbirth, while men are taught they mature after completing a quest. She encourages the graduates to think instead of becoming a woman 'through the chrysalis of education'. In message no. 2, she tells women to 'ask for money in your lives', explaining that 'the only language the status quo understands is money, votes and public embarrassment'. In message no. 3, Wolf states, 'Never cook for or sleep with anyone who routinely puts you down'. Her last message, however, speaks most clearly to her own struggle to find and defend her voice.

A Woman's Place 1992

Message No. 4: Become goddesses of disobedience... Young women tell me of injustices, from campus rape coverups to classroom sexism. But at the thought of confrontation, they freeze into niceness. We are told that the worst thing we can do is cause conflict, even in the service of doing right. Antigone is imprisoned. Joan of Arc burns at the stake. And someone might call us unfeminine!

... I began to ask each time: 'What's the worst that could happen to me if I tell this truth?' Unlike women in other countries, our breaking silence is unlikely to have us jailed, 'disappeared' or run off the road at night. Our speaking out will irritate some people, get us called bitchy or hypersensitive and disrupt some dinner parties. And then our speaking out will permit other women to speak, until laws are changed and lives are saved and the world is altered forever.

... Next time, ask: What's the worst that will happen? Then push yourself a little further than you dare. Once you start to speak, people will yell at you. They will interrupt you, put you down and suggest it's personal. And the world won't end.

And the speaking will get easier and easier. And you will find you have fallen in love with your own vision, which you may never have realized you had. And you will lose some friends and lovers, and realize you don't miss them.... And at last you'll know with surpassing certainty that only one thing is more frightening than speaking your truth. And that is not speaking.

Severn Cullis-Suzuki

Environmental Activist

When Severn Cullis-Suzuki was twelve years old, she travelled from Canada to Rio de Janeiro with the Environmental Children's Organization (ECO) to give a presentation at the 1992 United Nations Conference on Environment and Development. 'We are a group of twelve and thirteen year olds trying to make a difference,' she told her audience. 'We've raised all the money to come here ourselves, to come five thousand miles to tell you adults you *must* change your ways.' Cullis-Suzuki grew up in Vancouver, Canada, and describes in her speech her love for the outdoors – how she fishes for salmon with her father and dreams of visiting the rainforest. Her ambitions crystallized, however, once she became aware of the disastrous effects of climate change.

Cullis-Suzuki remains an environmental activist today, championing organizations that support a cleaner Canada, and encouraging students to speak up. In her Rio de Janeiro speech, she leveraged her unique position as a child speaking to adults – an emissary from generation future – to powerful effect. She is direct and unblinking in her assessment. 'I'm only a child and I don't have all the solutions, but I want you to realize, neither do you.' She speaks about consumer waste in Canada and makes a personal appeal to her listeners. 'Here, you may be delegates of your governments, business people, organizers, reporters or politicians – but really you are mothers and fathers, sisters and brothers, aunts and uncles – and *all* of you are someone's child.'

In my anger,
I am not blind, and in my fear,
I am not afraid of telling the
world how I feel.

Severn Cullis-Suzuki

Address to the United Nations Conference on Environment and Development 1992

Coming up here today, I have no hidden agenda. I am fighting for my future.

Losing my future is not like losing an election or a few points on the stock market.

I am here to speak for all generations to come.

I am here to speak on behalf of the starving children around the world whose cries go unheard.

I am here to speak for the countless animals dying across this planet, because they have nowhere left to go.

I am afraid to go out in the sun now because of the holes in our ozone.

I am afraid to breathe the air because I don't know what chemicals are in it.

I used to go fishing in Vancouver, my home, with my dad until just a few years ago we found the fish full of cancers.

And now we hear of animals and plants going extinct every day, vanishing forever. In my life, I have dreamt of seeing the great herds of wild animals, jungles and rainforests full of birds and butterflies, but now I wonder if they will even exist for my children to see.

Did you have to worry of these things when you were my age?

All this is happening before our eyes and yet we act as if we have all the time we want and all the solutions.

... I'm only a child yet I know we are all part of a family, five billion strong; in fact, 30 million species strong and borders and governments will never change that. I'm only a child yet I know we are all in this together and should act as one single world towards one single goal.

In my anger, I am not blind, and in my fear, I am not afraid of telling the world how I feel.

At school, even in kindergarten, you teach us how to behave in the world.

You teach us not to fight with others, to work things out, to respect others, to clean up our mess, not to hurt other creatures, to share and not be greedy.

Then why do you go out and do the things you tell us not to do?

Do not forget why you're attending these conferences, who you're doing this for.

We are your own children. You are deciding what kind of world we are growing up in. Parents should be able to comfort their children by saying "everything's going to be alright," "it's not the end of the world" and "we're doing the best we can."

But I don't think you can say that to us anymore. Are we even on your list of priorities?

My dad always says "you are what you do, not what you say".

Well, what you do makes me cry at night.

You grown-ups say you love us.

But I challenge you, please make your actions reflect your words.

The seal reads: SEAL OF THE CHEROKEE NATION · SEPT. 6, 1839

Wilma Mankiller
Principal Chief of the Cherokee Nation (1985–95)

Wilma Mankiller, the first female Principal Chief of the Cherokee Nation, was born in 1945. She was descended on her father's side from Georgia Cherokees evicted from their land in the 1830s and forced to march to Oklahoma on Andrew Jackson's 'Trail of Tears'. In her twenties, she became an activist and participated in an occupation of Alcatraz. Later, Mankiller returned to Oklahoma and led the Bell water project where she inspired the Bell community to build nearly twenty miles of waterline. That project, which is the subject of the award winning film, *Cherokee Word for Water*, led to Mankiller being elected deputy chief in 1983. In 1985 she became the principal chief. During her rise to leader, she was surprised to confront a deep-seated sexism within her community; she clashed often with the men on her tribal council. By the time of her death in 2010, however, she had served three terms as principal chief. She oversaw the growth of the nation from about 68,000 members to 170,000, championing causes including tribal education and women's rights.

In a commencement speech delivered at Northern Arizona University in 1992, Mankiller described, with amusement, being asked by a young man if he should call her 'Chiefette', because of her gender. The young man then asked about her last name. (The name 'Mankiller' comes from the Cherokee word for '"keeper of the village".) 'But that's not what I told this young man,' Mankiller jokes with the audience, 'I told him it was a nickname and I had earned it.'

Northern Arizona University Commencement Speech 1992

In American society it is always, 'They're going to solve that problem.' I don't know who 'they' are. I always tell our own people that I don't know who they are referring to. To me the only people who are going to solve our problems are ourselves – people like you and me....

There still exists in this country many negative stereotypes about black people, Latin people, and Asian people. God knows there are terrible stereotypes about Native Americans; these have to be overcome before we can move forward.

Sometimes I sit down with a diverse group of people in Oklahoma to work on some problem that we all have in common; it is almost like sitting down with people who have some kind of veil over their face or something. We all look at each other through this veil that causes us to see each other through these stereotypes. I think we need to lift back the veil and deal with each other on a more human level in order to continue to progress.

The minority population in this country is dramatically increasing, and that is a fact.... We need to find ways of dealing with each other and working with each other in much better ways.... I would urge all of you who are here today, both graduates and families, to examine the extent to which we hold those stereotypes about one another. And finally, I would hope my being here and spending just a couple of minutes with you today would help you to eliminate any stereotypes you might have about what a chief looks like.

Toni Morrison
Novelist

When passionate storyteller Toni Morrison accepted the
Nobel Prize in Literature in 1993, she began her speech with a
well-known parable, one that exists in many cultures: 'Once
upon a time there was an old woman.' In the version Morrison
told, the woman is blind, black, the descendent of slaves in
America, and living in a house on the outskirts of town. The
woman is clairvoyant, and one day a group of children decide
to test her powers. They approach in a group, and one of
them, holding out his hand, says 'Old woman, I hold in my
hand a bird. Tell me whether it is living or dead.'

From this deceptively simple beginning, Morrison, the
eighth woman – and the first black woman – to win the prize,
detailed an intricate theory of language. Morrison grew up in
Ohio and worked for many years as a book editor on the East
Coast before becoming a full time author. In novels including
The Bluest Eye, *Song of Solomon*, and *Beloved*, she explored
questions of race and the search for self. For Morrison, these
themes were best expressed through language, which
possesses an agency of its own. Words have real power, she
argued, with the ability not only to represent but to create
meaning. 'Word-work is sublime,' the old woman in Morrison's
speech thinks, 'because it is generative; it makes meaning
that secures our difference, our human difference – the way in
which we are like no other life.'

Nobel Lecture 1993

Speculation on what (other than its own frail body) that bird-in-the-hand might signify has always been attractive to me ... So I choose to read the bird as language and the woman as a practiced writer. She is worried about how the language she dreams in, given to her at birth, is handled, put into service, even withheld from her for certain nefarious purposes. Being a writer she thinks of language partly as a system, partly as a living thing over which one has control, but mostly as agency – as an act with consequences. So the question the children put to her: 'Is it living or dead?' is not unreal because she thinks of language as susceptible to death, erasure; certainly imperiled and salvageable only by an effort of the will. She believes that if the bird in the hands of her visitors is dead the custodians are responsible for the corpse. For her a dead language is not only one no longer spoken or written, it is unyielding language content to admire its own paralysis....

She is convinced that when language dies, out of carelessness, disuse, indifference and absence of esteem, or killed by fiat, not only she herself, but all users and makers are accountable for its demise. In her country children have bitten their tongues off and use bullets instead to iterate the voice of speechlessness, of disabled and disabling language.... But she knows tongue-suicide is not only the choice of children. It is common among the infantile heads of state and power merchants whose evacuated language leaves them with no access to what is left of their human instincts for they speak only to those who obey, or in order to force obedience.

The systematic looting of language can be recognized by the tendency of its users to forgo its nuanced, complex, mid-wifery properties for menace and subjugation. Oppressive language does more than represent violence; it is violence; does more than represent the limits of knowledge; it limits knowledge. Whether i t is obscuring state language or the faux-language of mindless media ... whether it is the malign language of law-without-ethics, or language designed for the estrangement of minorities, hiding its racist plunder in its literary cheek – it must be rejected, altered and exposed. It is the language that drinks blood, laps vulnerabilities, tucks its fascist boots under crinolines of respectability and patriotism as it moves relentlessly toward the bottom line and the bottomed-out mind. Sexist language, racist language, theistic language – all are typical of the policing languages of mastery, and cannot, do not permit new knowledge or encourage the mutual exchange of ideas.

Oppressive language does more than represent violence; it is violence...

Toni Morrison

Hillary Clinton

First Lady of the United States (1993–2001) and Politician

Before 2016, when Hillary Clinton's run for President of the United States sparked an international debate about women and political power, she spent years fighting to expand the rights of women and children. As First Lady from 1993 to 2001, while her husband, Bill Clinton, was president, she championed legislation on children's healthcare and helped create the Justice Department's Office on Violence Against Women. As Secretary of State, from 2009 to 2013, during Barack Obama's presidency, she stressed the link between national security and women's rights, an approach dubbed the 'Hillary Doctrine'. During the 2016 presidential election, bullied and belittled by her opponent Donald J. Trump (he famously called her a 'nasty woman'), she remained dignified and pragmatic. Although she ultimately lost, her determined run activated a broad swath of women in the United States and beyond.

In 1995, two years into her husband's presidency, Clinton spoke before delegates from 189 countries at the Fourth World Conference on Women, in Beijing. In her remarks she takes an unequivocal stance, declaring, 'women's rights are human rights, once and for all'. This line would be much quoted by women's rights advocates in the years to follow. 'The great challenge of this conference is to give voice to women everywhere whose experiences go unnoticed, whose words go unheard,' Clinton tells her audience. 'Those of us who have the opportunity to be here have the responsibility to speak for those who could not.'

Remarks for the United Nations Fourth World Conference on Women
1995

I believe that now, on the eve of a new millennium, it is time to break the silence.... it is no longer acceptable to discuss women's rights as separate from human rights.

These abuses have continued because, for too long, the history of women has been a history of silence. Even today, there are those who are trying to silence our words.

... It is a violation of human rights when babies are denied food, or drowned, or suffocated, or their spines broken, simply because they are born girls.

... when women are doused with gasoline, set on fire and burned to death because their marriage dowries are deemed too small.

... when individual women are raped in their own communities and when thousands of women are subjected to rape as a tactic or prize of war.

... when a leading cause of death worldwide among women ages 14 to 44 is the violence they are subjected to in their own homes.

... when young girls are brutalized by the painful and degrading practice of genital mutilation.

... when women are denied the right to plan their own families....

If there is one message that echoes forth from this conference, let it be that human rights are women's rights.... And women's rights are human rights, once and for all.

Wangari Maathai
Political Activist

In 2004, Wangari Maathai became the first African woman to win the Nobel Peace Prize. She began her acceptance speech by acknowledging her place in history. 'As the first African woman to receive this prize, I accept it on behalf of the people of Kenya and Africa, and indeed the world,' she said. 'I am especially mindful of women and the girl child. I hope it will encourage them to raise their voices and take more space for leadership.'

In 1977, Maathai founded the Green Belt Movement in Nairobi, Kenya. The grassroots organization's mission was to empower citizens through the planting of trees: it started with women.

'Throughout Africa, women are the primary caretakers,' Maathai explained in her Nobel lecture. 'As a result, they are often the first to become aware of environmental damage as resources become scarce.' She encouraged her audience to look to themselves, instead of 'outside' for solutions. Through her work, she came to understand environmental stewardship as intrinsically linked to democracy and peace. For Maathai, who adored nature as a child, the tree was both a practical solution and a symbol of a better world – one each individual has a stake in protecting.

Nobel Lecture 2004

So, together, we have planted over 30 million trees that provide fuel, food, shelter, and income to support [rural women's] children's education and household needs. The activity also creates employment and improves soils and watersheds. Through their involvement, women gain some degree of power over their lives.... This work continues.

... Although initially the Green Belt Movement's tree planting activities did not address issues of democracy and peace, it soon became clear that responsible governance of the environment was impossible without democratic space. Therefore, the tree became a symbol for the democratic struggle in Kenya. Citizens were mobilised to challenge widespread abuses of power, corruption and environmental mismanagement....

In 2002, the courage, resilience, patience and commitment of members of the Green Belt Movement, other civil society organizations, and the Kenyan public culminated in the peaceful transition to a democratic government and laid the foundation for a more stable society.

... It is 30 years since we started this work. Activities that devastate the environment and societies continue unabated. Today we are faced with a challenge that calls for a shift in our thinking, so that humanity stops threatening its life-support system....

I reflect on my childhood experience when I would visit a stream next to our home to fetch water for my mother. I would drink water straight from the stream.... I saw thousands of tadpoles: black, energetic and wriggling through the clear water.... This is the world I inherited from my parents.

Today, over 50 years later, the stream has dried up, women walk long distances for water, which is not always clean, and children will never know what they have lost. The challenge is to restore the home of the tadpoles and give back to our children a world of beauty and wonder.

J.K. Rowling
Novelist

By almost any standard, British author J.K. Rowling, the wizard behind Harry Potter, has achieved phenomenal success. Now part of a global franchise, *Harry Potter* books have been translated into sixty-eight languages, and sold over 400 million copies worldwide, making Rowling one of the wealthiest women in the UK. Born into a middle-class family near Gloucestershire, Rowling's ascent is an unlikely one. Living in Edinburgh in the early 1990s, several aimless years after graduation, Rowling considered herself an abject failure. Her short first marriage had ended, and she was unemployed, a single mother, and struggling financially. She felt she had let herself and her parents down. 'By every usual standard I was the biggest failure I knew,' she later recalled.

In a Harvard commencement speech delivered in 2008, Rowling took up the unexpected benefits of failure and the power of the imagination as her subject. She describes her struggle to find her voice in her fiction, and the fearlessness she found along the way. 'We do not need magic to change the world, we carry all the power we need inside ourselves already: we have the power to imagine better,' she said. She concluded with a line from Seneca, the Roman philosopher, which she discovered as an undergraduate still uncertain of her path and which has stuck with her through the years: 'As is a tale, so is life: not how long it is, but how good it is, is what matters.'

And so rock bottom became the solid foundation on which I rebuilt my life.

J.K. Rowling

Harvard University Commencement Speech 2008

So why do I talk about the benefits of failure? Simply because failure meant a stripping away of the inessential. I stopped pretending to myself that I was anything other than what I was, and began to direct all my energy into finishing the only work that mattered to me. Had I really succeeded at anything else, I might never have found the determination to succeed in the one arena I believed I truly belonged. I was set free, because my greatest fear had been realised, and I was still alive, and I still had a daughter whom I adored, and I had an old typewriter and a big idea. And so rock bottom became the solid foundation on which I rebuilt my life.

You might never fail on the scale I did, but some failure in life is inevitable. It is impossible to live without failing at something, unless you live so cautiously that you might as well not have lived at all – in which case, you fail by default.

Failure gave me an inner security that I had never attained by passing examinations. Failure taught me things about myself that I could have learned no other way. I discovered that I had a strong will, and more discipline than I had suspected; I also found out that I had friends whose value was truly above the price of rubies.

The knowledge that you have emerged wiser and stronger from setbacks means that you are, ever after, secure in your ability to survive. You will never truly know yourself, or the strength of your relationships, until both have been tested by adversity. Such knowledge is a true gift, for all that it is painfully won, and it has been worth more than any qualification I ever earned.

So given a Time Turner, I would tell my 21-year-old self that personal happiness lies in knowing that life is not a check-list of acquisition or achievement. Your qualifications, your CV, are not your life, though you will meet many people of my age and older who confuse the two. Life is difficult, and complicated, and beyond anyone's total control, and the humility to know that will enable you to survive its vicissitudes.

Angela Merkel

Chancellor of Germany (2005–)

In 2009, just before the twentieth anniversary of the fall of the Berlin Wall, German Chancellor Angela Merkel addressed the United States Congress in a speech that made the case for international cooperation. She began by recalling her experience growing up in the German Democratic Republic (GDR) – 'the part of Germany that was not free', as she described it – and how she overcame these limits to rise to the position of one of the most important leaders of the Western world – male or female. In her quiet, pragmatic way, Merkel has overseen Germany's transformation into an economic powerhouse, and has seen her popularity soar in the process.

In her speech, Merkel offers a stirring defence of globalization. She calls on world leaders to tear down 'the walls of the twenty-first century' – walls of intolerance and narrow self-interest. As the world becomes smaller, nations must work together in partnership, not isolation. She concludes with a reflection on Berlin's Freedom Bell, given to Germany by the United States in 1950; a link between two cultures. 'The Freedom Bell in Berlin is, like the Liberty Bell in Philadelphia, a symbol which reminds us that freedom does not come about of itself. It must be struggled for and then defended anew every day of our lives.'

Speech to the US Congress
2009

All things are possible, also in the 21st century, in the age of globalization. We back home in Germany know just as well as you do in America that many people are afraid of globalization. We do not just brush these concerns aside. We recognize the difficulties. And yet it is our duty to convince people that globalization is an immense global opportunity, for each and every continent, because it forces us to act together with others. The alternative to globalization would be shutting ourselves off from others, but this is not a viable alternative. It would lead only to isolation and therefore misery. Thinking in terms of alliances and partnerships on the other hand, is what will take us into a good future.

... That which brings Europeans and Americans closer together and keeps them close is a common basis of shared values. It is a common idea of the individual and his inviolable dignity. It is a common understanding of freedom in responsibility. This is what we stand for in the unique transatlantic partnership and in the community of shared values that is NATO.

This is what fills "Partnership in Leadership" with life, ladies and gentlemen.

This basis of values was what ended the Cold War, and it is this basis of values that will enable us to stand the tests of our times—and these tests we must stand.

... Even after the end of the Cold War we are thus faced with the task of tearing down the walls between different concepts of life, in other words the walls in people's minds that make it difficult time and again to understand one another in this world of ours. This is why the ability to show tolerance is so important. While, for us, our way of life is the best possible way, others do not necessarily feel that way. There are different ways to create peaceful coexistence. Tolerance means showing respect for other people's history, traditions, religion and cultural identity.

... Ladies and gentlemen, I am convinced that, just as we found the strength in the 20th century to tear down a wall made of barbed wire and concrete, today we have the strength to overcome the walls of the 21st century, walls in our minds, walls of short-sighted self-interest, walls between the present and the future.

Sheryl Sandberg
Chief Operating Officer at Facebook (2008–)

When Sheryl Sandberg's book, *Lean In: Women, Work, and the Will to Lead* was published in 2013, it immediately shot to the top of bestseller lists. In newspapers, radio programmes and television talk shows across the US and, eventually, abroad, the book sparked a public debate about ingrained sexism in the workplace, and the internal and external obstacles faced by professional women. Two years earlier, at a Barnard College commencement ceremony, Sandberg had given a speech that synthesized many of the book's key arguments. The chief operating officer of Facebook, and the first woman to sit on the company's board of directors, Sandberg advised the young women graduating to 'lean in' to their careers: to avoid holding back at work because they plan, someday, to start a family.

'As we sit here looking at this magnificent blue-robed class, we have to admit something that's sad but true: men run the world,' she said. 'Of 190 heads of state, nine are women. Of all the parliaments around the world, 13% of those seats are held by women.' The corporate world was not much different, she added. 'Corporate America top jobs, 15% are women; numbers which have not moved at all in the past nine years.' However Sandberg, who worked her way up the hierarchy at Google and then Facebook to become one of the most powerful women in Silicon Valley, believes this can change. 'But if all young women start to lean in, we can close the ambition gap right here, right now,' she said. 'Leadership belongs to those who take it. Leadership starts with you.'

Barnard College Commencement Speech 2011

Of course not everyone wants to jump into the workforce and rise to the top. Life is going to bring many twists and turns, and each of us, each of you, have to forge your own path. I have deep respect for my friends who make different choices than I do, who choose the really hard job of raising children full time, who choose to go part time, or who choose to pursue more nontraditional goals. These are choices that you may make some day, and these are fine choices.

But until that day, do everything you can to make sure that when that day comes, you even have a choice to make. Because what I have seen most clearly in my 20 years in the workforce is this:

Women almost never make one decision to leave the workforce. It doesn't happen that way. They make small little decisions along the way that eventually lead them there. Maybe it's the last year of med school when they say, I'll take a slightly less interesting specialty because I'm going to want more balance one day. Maybe it's the fifth year in a law firm when they say, I'm not even sure I should go for partner, because I know I'm going to want kids eventually.

These women don't even have relationships, and already they're finding balance, balance for responsibilities they don't yet have. And from that moment, they start quietly leaning back. The problem is, often they don't even realize it. Everyone I know who has voluntarily left a child at home and come back to the workforce— and let's face it, it's not an option for most people. But for people in this audience, many of you are going to have this choice. Everyone who makes that choice will tell you the exact same thing: You're only going to do it if your job is compelling.

If several years ago you stopped challenging yourself, you're going to be bored. If you work for some guy who you used to sit next to, and really, he should be working for you, you're going to feel undervalued, and you won't come back. So, my heartfelt message to all of you is, and start thinking about this now, do not leave before you leave. Do not lean back; lean in. Put your foot on that gas pedal and keep it there until the day you have to make a decision, and then make a decision. That's the only way, when that day comes, you'll even have a decision to make.

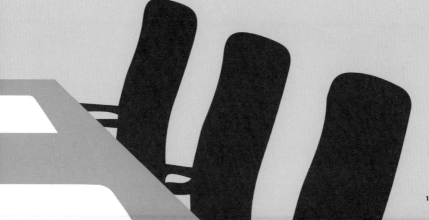

Ellen Johnson Sirleaf
President of Liberia (2006–18)

In 2005, Ellen Johnson Sirleaf was elected President of
Liberia. Africa's first elected female president, she inherited a
country suffering from the after-effects of a long and violent
civil war, during which rape and the use of child soldiers
proliferated. In 2011, Sirleaf, who studied at Harvard, shared
the Nobel Peace Prize with Leymah Gbowee, a Liberian
activist, and Tawakkol Karman, the Yemeni journalist and
activist, 'for their non-violent struggle for the safety of
women and women's rights to full participation in peace-
building work'. Sirleaf accepted the prize 'On behalf of all the
women of Liberia, the women of Africa, and women
everywhere in the world who have struggled for peace,
justice and equality'.

In her Nobel lecture, Sirleaf described her childhood in
Liberia, where she was raised by her parents and her
grandmothers to value a life of service. She outlined the
brutal toll a country at war takes on women and called
education for girls still 'under-funded and under-staffed'. 'Yet,
there is occasion for optimism and hope', she said. 'The
windows of closed chambers where men and women have
been unspeakably abused are being opened and the light is
coming in.' Referencing her co-laureates, she described
'three women linked by their commitment to change…. The
fact that we – two women from Liberia – are here today to
share the stage with a sister from Yemen speaks to the
universality of our struggle.'

Left: *Ellen Johnson Sirleaf*
Middle: *Leymah Gbowee*
Right: *Tawakkol Karman*

Nobel Lecture 2011

The Nobel Committee cannot license us three Laureates to speak for women. But it has provided us a platform from which to speak to women, around the globe, whatever their nationality, their color, their religion, or their station in life. It is you, my sisters, and especially those who have seen the devastation that merciless violence can bring, to whom I dedicate my remarks, and this Prize.

There is no doubt that the madness that wrought untold destruction in recent years in the Democratic Republic of Congo, in Rwanda, in Sierra Leone, in Sudan, in Somalia, in the former Yugoslavia, and in my own Liberia, found its expression in unprecedented levels of cruelty directed against women.

... Through the mutilation of our bodies and the destruction of our ambitions, women and girls have disproportionately paid the price of domestic and international armed conflict. We have paid in the currencies of blood, of tears, and of dignity.

Today, across the globe, women, and also men, from all walks of life are finding the courage to say, loudly and firmly, in a thousand languages, 'No more.' They reject mindless violence, and defend the fundamental values of democracy, of open society, of freedom, and of peace.

So I urge my sisters, and my brothers, not to be afraid. Be not afraid to denounce injustice, though you may be outnumbered. Be not afraid to seek peace, even if your voice may be small. Be not afraid to demand peace.

If I might thus speak to girls and women everywhere, I would issue them this simple invitation: My sisters, my daughters, my friends, find your voices!

The political struggles that our countries - Liberia, Yemen and others - have gone through will be meaningful only if the new-found freedom opens new opportunities for all. We are well aware that a new order, born of hunger for change, can easily fall back into the lawless ways of the past. We need our voices to be heard. Find your voice! And raise your voice! Let yours be a voice for freedom!

My sisters,
my daughters, my friends,
find your voices!

Ellen Johnson Sirleaf

Asmaa Mahfouz
Political Activist

In early 2011, amid unrest in Egypt during the last days of President Hosni Mubarak's thirty-year rule, a handful of protestors set themselves on fire in a startling demonstration against the government. Soon afterwards, Asmaa Mahfouz, a twenty-six-year-old youth activist living in Cairo, posted a video to her blog in which she asked her fellow Egyptians to join her in another, separate protest in Tahrir Square on 25 January. In the video, her fury and courage are on full display; she speaks confidently, staring directly into the camera. She recalls a previous demonstration against Mubarak, during which she was harassed by riot police: 'I posted that I, a girl, am going down to Tahrir Square, and I will stand alone.' Of the upcoming protest, she says, undaunted, 'I will not set myself on fire. If the security forces want to set me on fire, let them come and do it.'

Mahfouz's video soon went viral, attracting messages of solidarity from across Egypt and abroad. On 25 January, tens of thousands of Egyptians filled Tahrir Square. Violent protests roiled nearby cities as well, culminating in Mubarak's resignation on 11 February, 2011. The uprising fell in line with radical changes sweeping Egypt's neighbours: revolutions in Tunisia, Yemen, Libya, Syria, Bahrain and elsewhere are now collectively known as the Arab Spring. Mahfouz's words have been widely recognized for their role in inciting action. She leverages her identity as a woman by calling out men, specifically. She seems to say: If I can do it, why can't you?

The Vlog that Helped Spark the Egyptian Revolution 2011

I'm making this video to give you one simple message. We want to go down to Tahrir Square on January 25th. If we still have honor, and want to live in dignity on this land, we have to go down on January 25th. We'll go down and demand our rights, our fundamental human rights....

Whoever says women shouldn't go to protests because they will get beaten, let him have some honor and manhood and come with me on January 25th. Whoever says it's not worth it coz there will be only a handful of people, I want to tell him, you are the reason behind this and you are a traitor, just like the president or any security cop who beats us in the streets. Your presence with us will make a difference, a big difference!...

Bring 5 people, or 10 people; if each one of us manages to bring 5 or 10 to Tahrir Square and talk to people and tell them, this is enough! Instead of setting ourselves on fire, let us do something positive, it will make a difference, a big difference.

Never say there's no hope! Hope disappears only when you say there's no hope. So long as you come down with us, there will be hope. Don't be afraid of the government, fear none but God! God says that He "will not change the condition of a people until they change what is in themselves" (Qu'ran 13:11). Don't think you can be safe any more! None of us are! Come down with us, and demand your rights, my rights, your family's rights. I am going down on January 25th, and I will say "No" to corruption, "No" to this regime!

Manal al-Sharif
Women's Rights Activist

One evening in 2011, Manal al-Sharif was leaving her doctor's office in Al-Khobar, in eastern Saudi Arabia, when she began to feel unsafe. She could not find a ride home and a car had begun following her. She felt frustrated that, although she possessed an international driver's licence, she was not allowed to drive herself home in her own country. Following that incident, she created a short video in which she urged other Saudi women with licences to participate in a protest drive on 17 June 2011. She had learned that there was no official law barring women from driving, only an unofficial (and enforced) ban. She filmed a video of herself driving and posted it online, where it quickly went viral. The next day, al-Sharif was arrested and sent to jail for nine days.

Being the public face of what became known as the Women2Drive campaign was not easy for al-Sharif or her parents, who begged her to stop. But the movement was taking hold – other women were posting their own driving videos. In 2012, she was awarded the Václav Havel Prize for Creative Dissent and was invited to give a speech in Oslo. Her employer, a Saudi oil company, did not want her to go; al-Sharif resigned. After speaking, a fatwa was issued, and al-Sharif eventually emigrated to Australia. Yet her speech was a success, and in September 2017 she learned that the ban on Saudi women driving had been lifted. In her Oslo speech she recalled the first video she posted of herself driving. 'For me, the time of fear and silence was over… I was there to speak up for myself.'

The Drive for Freedom 2012

I always tell my mother, "they might handcuff me and send me behind jail bars, but I will never accept them putting cuffs on my mind. They can break my bones mom, but they can never break my soul".

Years of being passive, whispering complaints with so many years of signing petitions and waiting for a response that would never come, we decided finally that the time of silence is over. We took an action to change our reality. Waiting will result in nothing but more waiting and frustration.

But sadly even after a year later, women are still waiting for a miracle to happen to change their reality; they are still waiting for a royal decree to lift the ban on women driving. They don't know it will never come to them. It's up to them to take the key and go behind the wheel and just drive, as simple as it sounds, as simple as it is.

I believe that children cannot be free if their mothers are not free, parents cannot be free if their daughters are not free, husbands cannot be free if their wives cannot be free, society is nothing if women are nothing.

For me, freedom starts within. Here (my heart) I know I am free, but there, in Saudi, I am certain the struggle has just begun, the struggle will end but I am not sure when, the struggle is not about driving a car, the struggle is about being in the driver's seat of our own destiny, about being free not just to dream but free to live.

Julia Gillard

Prime Minister of Australia (2010–13)

In 2012, Julia Gillard, Australia's first female prime minister, spoke before the House of Representatives in an address quickly dubbed 'The Misogyny Speech'. In impassioned rhetoric and unfazed by the jeers of audience members, she argued against a motion by the Leader of the Opposition, Tony Abbott, to have the Speaker of the House, Peter Slipper, removed. Abbott maintained that a series of sexist text messages sent by Slipper made him unfit for office. In uncompromising language, which soon went viral, Gillard points to what she sees as the hypocrisy of Abbott's stance. What began as a medium-sized scandal in Australian politics touched off an international debate on sexism in political life: 'The Misogyny Speech' has been viewed online over three million times.

In her speech, Gillard reminds listeners of comments Abbott made regarding 'the housewives of Australia' doing the ironing ('Thank you for that painting of women's roles in modern Australia'), and of Abbott's views on abortion: 'I was very offended personally when the Leader of the Opposition, as Minister of Health, said, and I quote, "Abortion is the easy way out".' She calls him out for standing next to signs which described Gillard as a 'witch and a bitch', and for his friendship with Slipper. 'Well, this kind of hypocrisy must not be tolerated,' she said. 'The Leader of the Opposition should think seriously about the role of women in public life and in Australian society because we are entitled to a better standard than this.'

... I will not be lectured about sexism and misogyny by this man.

Julia Gillard

The Misogyny Speech 2012

Thank you very much Deputy Speaker and I rise to oppose the motion moved by the Leader of the Opposition. And in so doing I say to the Leader of the Opposition I will not be lectured about sexism and misogyny by this man. I will not. And the Government will not be lectured about sexism and misogyny by this man. Not now, not ever.

The Leader of the Opposition says that people who hold sexist views and who are misogynists are not appropriate for high office. Well, I hope the Leader of the Opposition has got a piece of paper and he is writing out his resignation. Because if he wants to know what misogyny looks like in modern Australia, he doesn't need a motion in the House of Representatives, he needs a mirror. That's what he needs.

... He has said, and I quote, in a discussion about women being under-represented in institutions of power in Australia, the interviewer was a man called Stavros. The Leader of the Opposition says 'If it's true, Stavros, that men have more power generally speaking than women, is that a bad thing?'

... This is the man from whom we're supposed to take lectures about sexism....

I was offended too by the sexism, by the misogyny of the Leader of the Opposition catcalling across this table at me as I sit here as Prime Minister, 'If the Prime Minister wants to, politically speaking, make an honest woman of herself....', something that would never have been said to any man sitting in this chair. I was offended when the Leader of the Opposition went outside in the front of Parliament and stood next to a sign that said 'Ditch the witch'.

... Misogyny, sexism, every day from this Leader of the Opposition. Every day in every way, across the time the Leader of the Opposition has sat in that chair and I've sat in this chair, that is all we have heard from him.

... Good sense, common sense, proper process is what should rule this Parliament.... [N]ot the kind of double standards and political game-playing imposed by the Leader of the Opposition now looking at his watch because apparently a woman's spoken too long. I've had him yell at me to shut up in the past, but I will take the remaining seconds of my speaking time to say to the Leader of the Opposition I think the best course for him is to reflect on the standards he's exhibited in public life, on theresponsibility he should take for his public statements; on his close personal connection with Peter Slipper, on the hypocrisy he has displayed in this House today.

Malala Yousafzai
Women's Education Activist

In 2012, fifteen-year-old Malala Yousafzai was on a bus in Pakistan, on her way home from school, when two members of the Taliban stopped the vehicle and shot at her three times. One bullet entered and exited her head, paralysing part of her face. She was airlifted to a hospital in Pakistan and then moved to Birmingham, England, where she received intensive treatment and survived. Yousafzai's story, and her exceptional courage, garnered international attention. Before the attack, she had become a vocal critic of the Taliban's ban on education for girls. In her hometown of Swat, she mourned the destruction of hundreds of schools. She appeared on local television to criticize the ban and, in 2009, began blogging anonymously about her experiences for the BBC.

In her acceptance speech for the Nobel Peace Prize, which she shared with the Indian activist Kailash Satyarthi, in 2014, she playfully acknowledged her age (she was the youngest person, and the first Pakistani, to receive the award). She joked about being the first Nobel Peace Prize recipient who still fights with her younger brothers. She pointed out the lack of a secondary school for girls in her hometown and reaffirmed her commitment to build one. Mainly, she used her platform to amplify the voices of others – she said the award belonged not just to her, but to all children who desire an education. 'Though I appear as one girl, one person, who is 5 foot 2 inches tall, if you include my high heels,' she said, 'I am not a lone voice, I am many.'

Nobel Lecture 2014

I have found that people describe me in many different ways.

Some people call me the girl who was shot by the Taliban.

And some, the girl who fought for her rights.

Some people, call me a 'Nobel Laureate' now.

However, my brothers still call me that annoying bossy sister. As far as I know, I am just a committed and even stubborn person who wants to see every child getting quality education, who wants to see women having equal rights and who wants peace in every corner of the world.

Education is one of the blessings of life – and one of its necessities. That has been my experience during the 17 years of my life. In my paradise home, Swat, I always loved learning and discovering new things. I remember when my friends and I would decorate our hands with henna on special occasions. And instead of drawing flowers and patterns we would paint our hands with mathematical formulas and equations....

But things did not remain the same. When I was in Swat, which was a place of tourism and beauty, suddenly changed into a place of terrorism. I was just ten that more than 400 schools were destroyed. Women were flogged. People were killed. And our beautiful dreams turned into nightmares.

Education went from being a right to being a crime.

Girls were stopped from going to school.

When my world suddenly changed, my priorities changed too.

I had two options. One was to remain silent and wait to be killed. And the second was to speak up and then be killed.

I chose the second one. I decided to speak up....

I tell my story, not because it is unique, but because it is not. It is the story of many girls....

... the so-called world of adults may understand it, but we children don't.

Why is it that countries which we call 'strong' are so powerful in creating wars but are so weak in bringing peace? Why is it that giving guns is so easy but giving books is so hard?...

Let this be the last time that a girl or a boy spends their childhood in a factory.

Let this be the last time that a girl is forced into early child marriage.

Let this be the last time that a child loses life in war.

Let this be the last time that we see a child out of school.

Let this end with us.

I tell my story,
not because it is unique,
but because it is not. It is the
story of many girls....

———————

Malala Yousafzai

Emma Watson
Actor and Activist

The British actor Emma Watson became an international
sensation when, at the age of eleven, she starred as the
precocious Hermione Granger in the first of the *Harry Potter*
films in 2001. Previously unknown (she had only acted in
school plays up to that point), she embarked on a career in
the public eye, making seven more blockbuster films adapted
from the fantastical novels penned by J.K. Rowling (see page
120). Towards the completion of the last Potter film, she
turned her attention towards education – she graduated from
Brown University, in Rhode Island, in 2014 – and women's
rights. As a Global Goodwill Ambassador for UN Women, she
has travelled to Uruguay, Malawi, and elsewhere to speak on
women's empowerment issues. In 2016, she started a popular
online feminist book club, 'Our Shared Shelf', which gained
100,000 members in a few weeks. A year earlier, *Time*
magazine named her to the TIME 100 list of the world's most
influential people, largely in reference to her work in support
of women's and girls' rights.

In 2014, at the United Nations in New York City, Watson
announced the launch of HeforShe, a campaign which aims to
make men a bigger part of the conversation surrounding
gender equality. Her speech, in which she spoke about the
negative impact of gender stereotypes on both men and
women, quickly went viral. In a moving passage, she
referenced Hillary Clinton's 1995 speech (see page 116), which
declared women's rights as human rights and noted how
much work remained. The word 'feminism', she explained, is
too often interpreted as 'man-hating'. Yet men are also
harmed by an unequal world. By framing the movement as an
inclusive one in which people of all genders have a stake,
HeforShe seeks to create new allies and feminist champions
across all parts of society.

HeForShe Launch Campaign 2014

We don't often talk about men being imprisoned by gender stereotypes but I can see that they are and that when they are free, things will change for women as a natural consequence.

If men don't have to be aggressive in order to be accepted women won't feel compelled to be submissive. If men don't have to control, women won't have to be controlled.

Both men and women should feel free to be sensitive. Both men and women should feel free to be strong.... It is time that we all perceive gender on a spectrum not as two opposing sets of ideals.

If we stop defining each other by what we are not and start defining ourselves by what we are—we can all be freer and this is what HeForShe is about. It's about freedom.

I want men to take up this mantle. So their daughters, sisters and mothers can be free from prejudice but also so that their sons have permission to be vulnerable and human too—reclaim those parts of themselves they abandoned and in doing so be a more true and complete version of themselves.

... We are struggling for a uniting word but the good news is we have a uniting movement. It is called HeForShe. I am inviting you to step forward, to be seen to speak up, to be the "he" for "she". And to ask yourself if not me, who? If not now, when?

I am inviting you to step forward, to be seen to speak up, to be the "he" for "she". And to ask yourself if not me, who? If not now, when?

Emma Watson

Jane Goodall

Ethologist and Conservationist

When Jane Goodall was a little girl, she was fascinated by where eggs come from. One afternoon, she hid so long in a chicken coop, hoping to solve the mystery, that her parents called the police. When her mother found her, she did not scold her. Instead, she listened as her daughter described her findings with excitement: a budding scientist. All her life, Goodall has cherished her enthusiasm for animals and the natural world. In 1960, aged just twenty-six, and without a college degree, she packed her bags for Gombe National Park, Tanzania, to undertake the first phase of what would become an ongoing study into wild chimpanzees that has lasted nearly sixty years. Her groundbreaking findings include the discovery that chimpanzees, like humans, use tools to forage for food. Goodall's early companion that made this pioneering trip possible? Her mother.

Since her first trip to Gombe, Goodall has accomplished an extraordinary amount as both a scientist and an activist. In 1965, she completed a PhD in Ethology, the study of animal behaviour, at the University of Cambridge (becoming one of the few people allowed to do so without an undergraduate degree). In 1977, she founded the Jane Goodall Institute, a global conservation organization, and, in 1991, she formed Roots & Shoots, empowering young people of all ages to become involved in projects to benefit their community, animals and the environment. Her determination to protect the environment was recognized in 2004, when she was named a Dame Commander of the Order of the British Empire. Ever the optimist, in 2016 she gave a lecture entitled 'Caring for the Earth – Reasons for Hope', in which she embodies a stunning answer to her own question: 'I'm one person, what can I do?'

Caring for the Earth – Reasons for Hope   2016

Every single one of us, every single one of us makes impact on this planet every single day. We cannot live through a day without making some kind of impact.

And we have a choice. Certainly everybody in this room has a choice. Some people don't have that much choice in their lives but we do. And if we start thinking about the consequences of the choices we make each day, the little things: what we buy, what we eat, what we wear, where did they come from, how was it made, did it result, the making of it, in cruelty to animals, was it child slave labour in a faraway place, did it harm the environment, that kind of thing, then we start making wiser choices. We can also ask ourselves do we really need it, is it necessary, do we have to buy this thing?

... If you think about everything, it's daunting. And I'm one person, what can I do? There's no point in doing anything because I'm helpless and hopeless. And so, people do nothing and they shut it all away, and they don't even think about it. They don't want to think about it because that would be depressing. So, it's this apathy that has to be overcome and I found particularly with young people that when they start realising that yes, me alone, I can't do anything but when there's hundreds or thousands or millions or maybe eventually billions of people all making the right choices, all trying to leave a slightly lighter ecological footprint, then we begin moving to the kind of world that we can be happier to leave to our descendants.

Michelle Obama

First Lady of the United States (2009–17) and Lawyer

Michelle Obama is one of the great speechmakers of our time. In her charisma and supreme command of an audience, she is every bit the equal of her husband, former United States president Barack Obama. In her eight years as First Lady, she used her position to champion causes from childhood obesity to LGBTQ rights. Raised on Chicago's South Side, Obama often speaks about where she comes from, and where she is going. As a teenager, she followed her older brother to Princeton University (neither of her parents graduated from college) and then went on to Harvard Law School. She met Barack as a young lawyer at the Chicago law firm Sidley & Austin, where she was his mentor.

In 2016, Obama addressed the Democratic National Convention, this time to voice her support for Hillary Clinton as the Democratic Party candidate in the upcoming presidential election. In an emotional speech, she looks back on her experience as a parent in the White House. She saw herself, she explains, as a role model for both her own daughters and for children all over the country. In this way, she draws a link between parenthood – particularly motherhood – and politics; a powerful (and savvy, given the context) endorsement of leadership positions for women. She begins by recalling the first day she saw Sasha and Malia, then seven and ten, in 'those black SUVs with all those big men with guns'. 'At that moment,' she says, 'I realized that our time in the White House would form the foundation for who they would become, and how well we managed this experience could truly make or break them.'

... our motto is, when they go low, we go high.

Michelle Obama

Speech at the Democratic National Convention 2016

That is what Barack and I think about every day as we try to guide and protect our girls through the challenges of this unusual life in the spotlight – how we urge them to ignore those who question their father's citizenship or faith. How we insist that the hateful language they hear from public figures on TV does not represent the true spirit of this country. How we explain that when someone is cruel, or acts like a bully, you don't stoop to their level – no, our motto is, when they go low, we go high.

With every word we utter, with every action we take, we know our kids are watching us. We as parents are their most important role models. And let me tell you, Barack and I take that same approach to our jobs as President and First Lady, because we know that our words and actions matter not just to our girls, but to children across this country – kids who tell us, "I saw you on TV, I wrote a report on you for school." Kids like the little black boy who looked up at my husband, his eyes wide with hope, and he wondered, "Is my hair like yours?"

... I want a President who will teach our children that everyone in this country matters – a President who truly believes in the vision that our founders put forth all those years ago: That we are all created equal, each a beloved part of the great American story. And when crisis hits, we don't turn against each other – no, we listen to each other. We lean on each other. Because we are always stronger together.

And I am here tonight because I know that that is the kind of president that Hillary Clinton will be. And that's why, in this election, I'm with her. You see, Hillary understands that the President is about one thing and one thing only – it's about leaving something better for our kids. That's how we've always moved this country forward – by all of us coming together on behalf of our children – folks who volunteer to coach that team, to teach that Sunday school class because they know it takes a village. Heroes of every color and creed who wear the uniform and risk their lives to keep passing down those blessings of liberty.

... That is the story of this country, the story that has brought me to this stage tonight, the story of generations of people who felt the lash of bondage, the shame of servitude, the sting of segregation, but who kept on striving and hoping and doing what needed to be done so that today, I wake up every morning in a house that was built by slaves and I watch my daughters – two beautiful, intelligent, black young women – playing with their dogs on the White House lawn. And because of Hillary Clinton, my daughters – and all our sons and daughters – now take for granted that a woman can be President of the United States.

Gloria Steinem
Journalist and Political Activist

In the collective understanding of the modern women's movement in the United States, perhaps no figure looms larger than Gloria Steinem. In the 1960s, she penned several high-profile feature articles (including one in which she went undercover as a Playboy Bunny) examining the state of women in America, before co-founding *Ms.* magazine in 1971. That same year, she spoke to members of the National Women's Political Caucus, which she helped launch, in an 'Address to the Women of America'. 'This is no simple reform. It really is a revolution,' she said.

On 21 January 2017, at the Women's March in Washington, D.C., she drew on her long history of activism in a speech delivered to some 500,000 people, many of them wearing pink pussyhats. She gave credit to her co-chairs, including Dolores Huerta and LaDonna Harris ('the Golden oldies, right?'), and praised the event, which took place the day after President Trump's inauguration, as a 'women-led, inclusive march'. 'I've been thinking about the uses of a long life, and one of them is you remember when things were worse,' she said, recalling the assassinations of Martin Luther King, Jr., and Malcolm X. Then she turned her attention to the future: 'Trump and his handlers have found a fox for every chicken coop in

Washington, and a Twitter finger must not become a trigger finger.' At the inauguration, Trump 'said he was with the people. Indeed, he was the people,' she recalled. 'To paraphrase a famous quote, I just have to say, "I have met the people, and you are not them." We are the people.'

Women's March Speech 2017

Just this march in Washington today required 1,000 more buses than the entire Inauguration. A thousand more buses. And I was just talking with people from our many sister marches, including the one in Berlin, and they asked me to send a special message: 'We in Berlin know that walls don't work.'

And remember Poland where last month the government passed an anti-abortion law and six million women turned out in the streets and they had to change it. We are the people. We have people power and we will use it. All the power that you tried to eliminate. For instance, you tried to eliminate the Congressional Ethics Committee. You had to reinstate it, right? Because of people power. Because this, this, is the other side of the downside. This is an outpouring of energy and true democracy like I have never seen in my very long life. It is wide in age. It is deep in diversity. And remember the constitution does not begin with 'I, the president'. It begins with 'We, the people'.

So don't try to divide us. Do not try to divide us. If you force Muslims to register, we will all register as Muslims. I know that there are women here from corporations and media and all kinds of places that make it kind of risky for you to say what you care about, what you feel, and what you support. And there are women here, I know, who have survived a national and global sex industry that profiteers from body invasion. We are united here for bodily integrity. If you cannot control your body from the skin in, you cannot control it from the skin out, you cannot control your lives, our lives. And that means that the right to decide whether and when to give birth without government interference.

We are here and around the world for a deep democracy that says we will not be quiet, we will not be controlled, we will work for a world in which all countries are connected. God may be in the details, but the goddess is in connections. We are at one with each other, we are looking at each other, not up. No more asking daddy.

We are linked. We are not ranked. And this is a day that will change us forever because we are together. Each of us individually and collectively will never be the same again. When we elect a possible president we too often go home. We've elected an impossible president, we're never going home. We're staying together. And we're taking over.

We are the people.
We have people power
and we will use it.

Gloria Steinem

Beatrice Fihn

Executive Director of the International Campaign to Abolish Nuclear Weapons (2014–)

When the Nobel Prize Committee called to inform Beatrice Fihn, the Executive Director of the International Campaign to Abolish Nuclear Weapons (ICAN), that her organization had won the 2017 Nobel Peace Prize, she thought it was a joke. Based in a small office in Geneva, ICAN had been working on the first global treaty to ban nuclear weapons since 2007. A decade later, the United Nations formally adopted the proposal and ICAN continued collecting signatures from eligible member states. (Fifty countries must ratify the document for it to take effect; the nine nations holding nuclear weapons boycotted the negotiations.) In a policy area historically dominated by men, the Swedish Fihn has made her voice heard, becoming a figurehead for the cause. 'We are a movement for rationality. For democracy. For freedom from fear,' she has said.

In her Nobel lecture, Fihn argued that 'We citizens are living under the umbrella of falsehoods. These weapons are not keeping us safe, they are contaminating our land and water, poisoning our bodies and holding hostage our right to life.' She called on nations with robust nuclear programmes to disarm, and painted the decision to support the treaty as 'a choice between the two endings: the end of nuclear weapons or the end of us'. 'It is not naive to believe in the first choice,' she maintained. 'It is not idealistic to believe in life over fear from destruction; it is a necessity.'

Nobel Lecture 2017

At dozens of locations around the world – in missile silos buried in our earth, on submarines navigating through our oceans, and aboard planes flying high in our sky – lie 15,000 objects of humankind's destruction.

Perhaps it is the enormity of this fact, perhaps it is the unimaginable scale of the consequences, that leads many to simply accept this grim reality. To go about our daily lives with no thought to the instruments of insanity all around us.

For it is insanity to allow ourselves to be ruled by these weapons. Many critics of this movement suggest that we are the irrational ones, the idealists with no grounding in reality. That nuclear-armed states will never give up their weapons.

But we represent the only rational choice. We represent those who refuse to accept nuclear weapons as a fixture in our world, those who refuse to have their fates bound up in a few lines of launch code.

Ours is the only reality that is possible. The alternative is unthinkable.

The story of nuclear weapons will have an ending, and it is up to us what that ending will be.

Will it be the end of nuclear weapons, or will it be the end of us?

One of these things will happen.

The only rational course of action is to cease living under the conditions where our mutual destruction is only one impulsive tantrum away.

Left to right: *Alicia Garza, Opal Tometi, Michelle Obama, Angela Davis*

Alicia Garza
Activist and Writer

In 2013, Alicia Garza was working as a community organizer in California when news broke that a jury had acquitted George Zimmerman in the death of the African-American teenager Trayvon Martin. Garza, who saw in Martin something of her little brother, expressed her grief in a Facebook post entitled 'a love letter to black people'. 'Black people. I love you. I love us. Our lives matter,' she wrote. Garza's friend and fellow organizer, Patrisse Khan-Cullors, added a hashtag and #BlackLivesMatter, the movement, was born. Since then, Black Lives Matter activists have founded dozens of local chapters and participated in protests around the United States and abroad, demonstrating against police brutality and systemic violence against black Americans.

Garza, who was born in 1981, often works behind the scenes (she believes in a flat organizational structure). Still, she is looked up to by many as a leader of a social movement with broad implications for race relations in America and elsewhere. In 2017, she gave a commencement speech at San Francisco State University, which she dedicated to a long line of powerful black women who came before her. She tells her audience that she would not be standing in front of them without the persistence and strength of black women, including her mother. Identifying as a queer woman herself, Garza has created space for voices outside of the mainstream. She ends with a question, which carries with it echoes of Sojourner Truth's sentiments and functions as both a rebuke and a call to action: 'Who does she think she is, that Black woman?'

This is an ode to the potential and the possible.

Alicia Garza

An Ode to Black Women 2017

This is an ode to Black women—because Black women are magic.

This is an ode to the Black women who persisted and the Black women who helped them each and every step of the way.

Were it not for a Black woman from the Midwest who could do anything a man could do and definitely do it better.

Were it not for that same Black woman getting pregnant with me and not being quite sure how she was gonna do it but she did it anyway.

... I would not be standing here today.

Were it not for Black women, there would be no Underground Railroad, no one to campaign against Black bodies swinging from trees like strange fruit, there would be no protest songs like the ones that came from the toes through the womb up through the lungs and out of the brilliant mind and mouth of Nina Simone.

... There would be no America were it not for Black women.

... Were it not for Black women like Dr. Dorothy Tsuruta and Dr. Dawn Elissa Fisher and Lynette Schwartz and Patrisse Cullors and Ada Bogan Trawick and Myrtle Buckhaulter and June Jordan and Barbara Smith and Lateefah Simon and Harriet Tubman and Malaika Parker and Angela Davis and Ericka Huggins and Linda Burnham and Diane Nash and Ella Baker and Brittney Cooper and Sojourner Truth and Ida B. Wells and Audre Lorde and Nina Simone and Mya Hall and Penny Proud and Patricia Hill Collins and Jessie Powell and Betty Higgins and Joanne Abernathy and Emma Harris and Espanola Jackson and Islan Nettles and Assata Shakur and Renisha McBride and Janetta Johnson and Kimberle Crenshaw and Janet Mock and Miss Major Griffin Gracy and dream hampton and Michelle Obama and MaeEtta Buckhaulter and Korryn Gaines and so many others whose names I may never know to speak but whose spirits course through my blood ... there would be no me no you no us no civilized society of which we speak.

We, I, you and me—we owe EVERYTHING to Black women.

Thank any and every god you want.

For the resilience.
Determination.
Audacity.
Persistence.
Dedication.
Power.
Presence.
Willpower.

And the lifting up of all of us all the time without hesitation or apology or the need to talk about all of us (cuz we been telling y'all that forever now, let's move forward) we just DO for all of us.

This is an ode to the potential and the possible....

Maya Lin
Sculptor and Architect

When American sculptor and architect Maya Lin addressed the graduates of New York's School of Visual Arts, class of 2018, she recalled her own commencement ceremony. She was distracted – she had just won the competition to design the Vietnam Veterans Memorial in Washington, D.C. Bold and minimalist, the memorial was completed in 1982, when Lin was in her early twenties. Widely regarded as one of the most important monuments of our time, it receives over five million visitors each year.

The memorial's success, however, was not always a given. It was shocking from the get-go. Her critics were unconvinced that someone so young – hardly out of school – and a woman as well, could pull off such a high-profile commission. In addition, everyone wanted to weigh in on her design, including male mentors with the weight of years of experience behind them. Yet Lin, who has since achieved international success as an artist and designer, stuck to her vision ('Youth gives us a sense of being invincible'). In her speech, she describes her own fears and anxieties about the artistic life and the 'singular' creative process, advising the graduates to move past self-doubt by embracing intuition. She tells them, '... you should not be afraid to offend anyone, to question everything, to reinvent yourself and to rethink the world.'

Believe that your one voice can make a difference.

_____

Maya Lin

SVA Commencement Address 2018

I believe everyone has a role and a responsibility to make the world a better place. Because the alternative is for us to help make the world a worse place, or to stand by and do nothing.

I believe that how you choose to relate, respond, and try to shape your time is very much a part of your evolution as an artist. Art can be both a leader and a mirror of the time we live in. Artists can see things that others can't.

We can present the world in a new light and get others to see a new truth, a new future. We can help to imagine and create a different world. Don't be afraid to get involved, don't be afraid to care. Believe that your one voice can make a difference. May you never lose that, that passion, that drive, that poetry.

I am struggling on new works all the time, trying to find new ideas and give them shape. It is the same struggle for all of us. And you are not alone....

And now, as you graduate here today, you are becoming part of a larger artistic community. One that stretches back into time, that creates a dialogue, a conversation with your fellow humans through all times.

I see it as a collective creative consciousness. Through art we know how people saw their world a thousand years ago. And through our art people a thousand years from now will see us.

I think it is amazing that William Shakespeare's words written four hundred years ago can still make us cry or laugh. Or that I stood in front of Picasso's Guernica in absolute silent awe....

How will your works be read and felt one hundred years from today? Or one thousand years from today? So today I ask you to become part of that conversation and to find your voice in this wondrous creative continuum. And I ask you, what would you like to say?

More Women to Inspire

The difficulty in compiling an anthology such as this is selecting those speeches to include and – necessarily – those to be left out. History is packed full of examples of inspiring women speaking up for the causes they believe in, from empresses and queens defending their right to rule in a patriarchal society to pioneering scientists and inventors working on the fringes of the establishment. And continuing right up to the present day are brave new voices – such as eighteen-year-old Emma González, the American activist who spoke passionately about the need for gun control in the wake of the February 2018 Stoneman Douglas High School shooting in Florida – who strikingly illustrate how impactful our voices can be.

The majority of speeches in this collection are post-1830s. This decade was the point at which the fight for women's rights in the Western world ushered women on to the public stage – a sphere in which previously they had been largely absent. Further back, a key difficulty for the researcher of women's speeches is the scarcity of accurate recordings of such events. There are many women – philosophers, leaders, writers, activists – who we know spoke in public, yet their exact words have been lost to the passage of time. While this precluded their inclusion in this collection, these women are a powerful example of the strong lineage of eloquent women who we can look back on to inspire us today.

The speeches in So Here I Am are intended to inspire and empower, and it is my hope that they will leave you wanting much more. Look up some of the women below: read their stories, listen to their speeches on YouTube, follow them on Twitter, and be energized by these impassioned orators.

Sappho, Greek Poet, c. 610–c. 570 BC

Greek poet Sappho was famous for her lyric poetry, most of which survives only in fragments. Much of her life is a mystery, but her prolific writing, which celebrated the lives, thoughts and passions of women, was greatly admired in antiquity, as she is to this day. The modern use of the term 'lesbian' to refer to erotic love between women is an allusion to Sappho (who lived on the Greek island Lesbos), as it is commonly thought (though still debated) by modern scholars that her poetry was homoerotic.

Hortensia, Roman Heroine, 1st century BC

Best known for her oration, delivered in the Roman Forum, opposing plans to tax the property of 1,400 wealthy women. The tax was to raise money for the war against murdered dictator Julius Caesar's assassins; Hortensia argued against such a levy on those who had no part in instigating or sustaining the conflict.

Boudicca, Queen of the Iceni, fl. AD 60

Following the annexation of the Iceni kingdom on the death of her husband, this ancient queen of a British tribe raised a rebellion against Roman rule, razing modern-day Colchester, St Albans and London to the ground.

Hypatia, Mathematician and Astronomer, c. 355–415

A leading mathematician, astronomer and philosopher, Hypatia lived at a particularly turbulent time in Alexandria's history. She is recorded as having been a popular teacher, attracting large audiences to hear her lectures on philosophy.

Eleanor of Aquitaine, Queen Consort of France and England, c. 1122–1204

Perhaps the most influential woman in medieval Europe, Eleanor of Aquitaine was an important patron of the arts as well as playing an active role in government. Eleanor's fifteen-year marriage to Louis VII of France was annulled in 1152 and two-months later she married Henry of Anjou. In 1154 Henry became Henry II of England; Eleanor was instrumental in helping to manage her husband's empire, travelling between England and France. In

1173 she sided with two of her sons in a plot against Henry and was imprisoned for her role in the attempted uprising. On his father's death in 1189, Richard I ordered the release of his mother who once again became a central figure in politics, acting as Regent in 1190 during Richard's crusade to the Holy Land.

St. Joan of Arc, French Heroine, c. 1412–31

A French peasant girl, Joan of Arc showed formidable courage when she persuaded the dauphin Charles (later Charles VII) to trust her to lead his troops against the English during the Hundred Years' War. Joan believed herself to be under divine guidance, and won important victories for the French, most notably at Patay, and in securing the coronation of Charles. She was captured in 1430, tried for heresy and executed.

Olympe de Gouges, Writer and Social Reformer, 1748–93

A prolific social activist and writer, de Gouges campaigned on issues including divorce, maternity hospitals and the rights

St. Joan of Arc

Hypatia

Boudicca

of unmarried mothers. In 1791 she published a pamphlet entitled 'Déclaration des droits de la femme et de la citoyenne' ('Declaration of the Rights of Woman and of the [Female] Citizen'). A supporter of the Girondins during the French Revolution, she was executed following their fall in 1793.

Mary Wollstonecraft, Writer and Feminist, 1759–97

Now recognized as a trailblazer in the women's rights movement, Wollstonecraft's most important work was the 1792 A Vindication of the Rights of Woman. In this, she argued for the wholesale reform of the educational system to equip women for employment and independent living.

Qiu Jin, Feminist Poet and Revolutionary, 1875–1907

During the unstable final years of the Qing government, Qiu Jin was a leading figure in the new wave of feminists who aligned women's rights with political revolution. Defying gender and class norms of the time, Qiu Jin unbound her feet, cross-dressed, and left her husband and children to travel to Japan and pursue an education. She

established the Chinese Women's Journal and wrote and spoke extensively on issues such as foot binding and arranged marriages. Executed by Qing troops in 1907, she is regarded as a revolutionary martyr by many in China.

Sarojini Naidu, Political Activist, Feminist and Poet, 1879–1949

Inspired by Mahatma Gandhi's non-cooperation movement, Naidu was a vocal campaigner for India's Congress movement. In 1925 she became the first Indian female President of the National Congress, travelling in eastern Africa, South Africa and North America to further the cause and lecture. Following independence, she served as governor of the United Provinces (modern-day Uttar Pradesh) from 1947 until her death. Today, Naidu's birthday is celebrated as Women's Day throughout India.

Dolores Ibárruri, Spanish Political Leader, 1895–1989

Known as 'La Pasionaria' ('The Passionflower'), Ibárruri was a vocal member of the Spanish Communist Party,

Emma González

Maya Angelou

jailed several times for her political activities. In a famous speech during the Spanish Civil War, she raised the rallying cry of 'No parasán!' – 'They shall not pass'. On Franco's victory, Ibárruri left Spain and travelled to Russia, where she remained active as the General Secretary of the Central Committee of the Communist Party of Spain. She returned to her home country in 1977.

Rachel Carson, Biologist, 1907–64

Carson wrote extensively on environmental pollution and marine biology. Her 1962 book, Silent Spring, became an international best seller and greatly increased awareness of environmental issues. Carson's pioneering work led to the creation of the US Environmental Protection Agency, and she was posthumously awarded the Presidential Medal of Freedom.

Simone de Beauvoir, Writer and Philosopher, 1908–86

A member of the existentialist intellectuals in France, in 1949 de Beauvoir wrote Le Deuxième Sexe (The Second Sex).

Recognized as a seminal feminist work, the book sought to answer the question: 'what is woman?'

Maya Angelou, Poet, Writer and Actress, 1928–2014

Maya Angelou's career saw incredible success as a writer of autobiographies, poetry and screenplays. She won a National Book Award Nomination for her first autobiography, I Know Why the Caged Bird Sings (1969), became one of the first African-American women to have a screenplay produced as a feature film with Georgia, Georgia, and performed 'On the Pulse of Morning' at Bill Clinton's inauguration as US President in 1993. Much-loved and respected, Angelou received the Presidential Medal of Freedom in 2010 from Barack Obama.

Betty Friedan, Author and Feminist, 1921–2006

Friedan was best known as the author of The Feminist Mystique, an incredibly influential work of feminist literature. Having interviewed many housewives, Friedan challenged the view that the

Simone de Beauvoir

Qiu Jin

designated role of wife and mother held the total fulfilment that society promoted. She also co-founded the National Organization for Women, campaigning to help women improve their lives in a variety of areas.

Billie Jean King, Tennis Player, b. 1943

Former World Number 1 tennis professional, Billie Jean King famously defeated Bobby Riggs, also a former World Number 1 player, in a 1973 match dubbed the 'Battle of the Sexes'. Following a playing career in which she won 39 Grand Slam titles, King has become an outspoken advocate for social justice and equality.

Benazir Bhutto, Prime Minister of Pakistan, 1953–2007

The first female leader of a Muslim country, Benazir Bhutto served two terms as Prime Minister of Pakistan. In a tumultuous political period, Bhutto, as leader of the Pakistan People's Party (PPP), found herself frequently under house arrest, lived in exile for a number of years and faced allegations of corruption while in government. In 1995, at the United Nations Conference on Women, Bhutto gave an eloquent address in which she demonstrated how the fundamental teachings of Islam protect and enshrine the rights of women.

Marie Colvin, Journalist, 1956–2012

War and foreign affairs correspondent Marie Colvin repeatedly put her life at risk to travel right to the heart of conflicts. Suffering the loss of one eye and later the loss of her life through her work, Colvin was always committed to bringing to light the true effects of war on the civilians affected by it. In 2010, Colvin spoke

movingly about the motivation of journalists to report on conflicts – even when it meant putting themselves in danger – at a service to commemorate reporters and support staff who had lost their lives during conflict.

Chimamanda Ngozi Adichie, Author, b. 1977

Having found great success in writing such novels as Half of a Yellow Sun (2006) and Americanah (2013), which were influenced by her Nigerian roots, Adichie also famously gave the 2012 TEDx Talk 'We Should All Be Feminists', which she later adapted into an essay. The speech – the author's second TED Talk – captured the attention of people around the world, with the slogan 'We Should All Be Feminists' emblazoned on t-shirts by fashion house Dior and quotes featured in Beyoncé's 2013 song '***Flawless'.

Emma González, b. 1999

In 2018 the world was shocked by the shooting at Stoneman Douglas High School in Parkland, Florida. In the wake of the tragedy, student survivors rose up eloquently to advocate gun control legislation in the United States. Eighteen-year-old González emerged as a leading figure in the movement, co-founding the gun control group Never Again MSD and becoming an outspoken activist for the cause. At the March for Our Lives (which she helped to organize), González gave a moving tribute to her fellow students who had lost their lives.

Read All About It!

Although women have typically been left out of collections of 'world changing speeches' – with a few rare exceptions – the history of pioneers in women's rights and inspirational women across the fields of politics, civil rights, science and technology, arts, sports and more, is a rich seam of research. Below are just some of the fascinating resources I drew inspiration from while writing this book - your starting point for a mind-opening feminist reading list, if you will:

A Room of One's Own, **Virginia Woolf** (Penguin Classics)

A Vindication of the Rights of Woman, **Mary Wollstonecraft** (Penguin Classics)

Dead Feminists: Historic Heroines in Living Color, **Chandler O'Leary and Jessica Spring** (Sasquatch Books)

Lean In: Women, Work, and the Will to Lead, **Sheryl Sandberg** (W.H. Allen)

Men Explain Things to Me: And Other Essays, **Rebecca Solnit** (Granta)

Modern Women: 52 Pioneers, **Kira Cochrane** (Frances Lincoln)

The Beauty Myth: How Images of Beauty are Used Against Women, **Naomi Wolf** (Vintage)

The Feminist Promise: 1792 to the Present, **Christine Stansell** (Modern Library)

The Feminist Mystique, **Betty Friedan** (Penguin Classics)

The Second Sex, **Simone de Beauvoir** (Vintage Classics)

We Should All Be Feminists, **Chimamanda Ngozi Adichie** (Fourth Estate)

Women & Power: A Manifesto, Mary Beard (Profile Books)

Credits

Elizabeth I With permission of the British Library, shelfmark: Harley 6798, f.87.

Fanny Wright Wright, Frances, *Course of Popular Lectures; with Three Addresses on Various Public Occasions, and A Reply to the Charges Against the French Reformers of 1789*, New York: Office of the Free Enquirer, 1829, pp. 41–62.

Maria Stewart Stewart, Maria W. Miller, *Meditations From the Pen of Mrs. Maria W. Stewart: (widow of the Late James W. Stewart,) Now Matron of the Freedmen's Hospital, and Presented In 1832 to the First African Baptist Church and Society of Boston, Mass.*, Washington: Enterprise Publishing Company, 1879.

Angelina Grimké Webb, Samuel, *History of Pennsylvania Hall, which was Destroyed by a Mob, on the 17th of May, 1838*, Philadelphia: Merrihew and Gunn, 1838.

Sojourner Truth *Anti-slavery bugle.* [volume] (New-Lisbon, Ohio) 21 June 1851. *Chronicling America: Historic American Newspapers.* Lib. of Congress.

Victoria Woodhull Woodhull, Victoria C., Lucy Stone, and National American Woman Suffrage Association Collection. '"And the truth shall make you free": a speech on the principles of social freedom, delivered in Steinway Hall', New York: Woodhull, Claflin & Co, 1871. PDF retrieved from the Library of Congress, <www.loc.gov/item/09008216/>.

Sarah Winnemucca Sally Zanjani Papers, 2013–04. Special Collections, University Libraries, University of Nevada, Reno.

Elizabeth Cady Stanton Library of Congress, Rare Book and Special Collections Division, National American Woman Suffrage Association Collection.

Mary Church Terrell Originally published in *The Independent*, January 24, 1907. Reprinted from *American Speeches: Political Oratory from Abraham Lincoln to Bill Clinton*, The Library of America, 2006, pp. 204–12.

Ida B. Wells *Proceedings of the National Negro Conference, 1909, New York, May 31 and June 1*, New York, 1909, pp. 174–179.

Countess Markievicz 'Women, Ideals and the Nation: A Lecture Delivered to the Students' National Literary Society, Dublin, by Constance de Markievicz', Dublin: Inghinidhe na h-Eireann, 1909. Text originated from Digital Library@ Villanova University. Creative Commons Attribution-ShareAlike 3.0 Unported (CC BY-SA 3.0).

Marie Curie © The Nobel Foundation 1911.

Emmeline Pankhurst Pankhurst, Emmeline, 'Verbatim report of Mrs. Pankhurst's speech; delivered Nov. 13, 1913 at Parsons' Theatre, Hartford, Conn.', Connecticut Woman Suffrage Association, 1913.

Nellie McClung Royal BC Museum and Archives, MS-0010, Box 20, File 3.

Jutta Bojsen-Møller Originally published in *Silkeborg Avis. Midt-Jyllands Folketidende* (1872–1974), June 7, 1915. Available from Mediestream. Translated by Tim Davies for Quarto Publishing Plc.

Emma Goldman For historical context and significance, including the address to the jury, see *Emma Goldman: Democracy Disarmed 1917–1919* (Stanford University Press, 2019), the fourth volume of the series *Emma Goldman: A Documentary History of the American Years 1890–1919*. See also www.lib.berkeley.edu/goldman/pdfs/Speeches-AddresstotheJury.pdf, www.lib.berkeley.edu/goldman, and www.archive.org/details/emmagoldmanpapers

Hillary Clinton First Lady's Office and First Lady's Press Office, "Speeches - Beijing & Ulaambaatar [Mongolia]," *Clinton Digital Library*, accessed October 30, 2018, **https://clinton. presidentiallibraries.us/items/show/2655.**

Wangari Maathai © The Nobel Foundation 2004.

J.K. Rowling Very Good Lives: Copyright © J.K. Rowling, 2008.

Angela Merkel As published on **bundesregierung.de.**

Sheryl Sandberg © Sheryl Sandberg & Dave Goldberg Family Foundation, all rights reserved.

Ellen Johnson Sirleaf © The Nobel Foundation 2011.

Asmaa Mahfouz Reprinted by permission of © Asmaa Mahfouz. Translated by Iyad el-Baghdadi.

Manal al-Sharif Reprinted by permission of Manal al-Sharif.

Julia Gillard As published on **juliagillard.com.au.**

Malala Yousafzai © The Nobel Foundation 2014.

Emma Watson © Emma Watson.

Jane Goodall Reprinted by permission of Jane Goodall PhD, DBE; Founder – the Jane Goodall Institute & UN Messenger of Peace. **www. janegoodall.org www.rootsandshoots.org**

Michelle Obama 'Remarks by the First Lady at the Democratic National Convention', The White House, Office of the First Lady, July 25, 2016. As published on **obamawhitehouse.archives.gov.**

Gloria Steinem Reprinted by permission of Gloria Steinem.

Beatrice Fihn © The Nobel Foundation 2017.

Alicia Garza Reprinted by permission of Alicia Garza.

Maya Lin Reprinted by permission of Maya Lin.

Acknowledgements

Sincere thanks to Philippa Wilkinson and Laura Bulbeck for their thoughtful edits and patient work wrangling these speeches. Thanks to Camila Pinheiro for her brilliant illustrations, which made the book come alive, and Isabel Eeles for her beautiful design work. Thanks especially to Helene Remiszewska who was invaluable as a fact-checker and all-around support. Thanks to the many experts who helped with context and clarity along the way: Judith A. Byfield, Cari Carpenter, Elizabeth Eames, Cheryl Johnson-Odim, Carolyn Sorisio, Christine Stansell, and Susan Stryker. Thanks to my inspiring colleagues at *The New Yorker*, for their encouragement and good-cheer, especially Susan Morrison, Lizzie Widdicombe, Nick Trautwein, Hannah Wilentz, Rachel Lipstein, Jeanie Riess, and Nimal Eames-Scott. Thank you to all the outspoken (and well-spoken) women in my life: Maureen McLane, Monika Woods, Beth Schepens, Katherine Dunn, Aditi Shah, Raven Jensen, Lindsay Gellman, Danielle Manno, Anabel Wold, Alex Carter, Alison Brown, Michelle Roginsky, Danielle Hartounian, Melody Rabe, Sanette Sloan, Hope Brimelow, Paige Birnbaum, Arianna Reiche, Eliza Doherty, Lucy Warburton, Lindsay Yellen, and many more. Thank you to my grandmothers, from whom I've learned so much, and to Nell, George, and Phil Hourdakis, for their support. Finally, thanks to my parents, Carrie and Ryan, and my brother, Brett, who make everything possible. And to Alex, who makes it all more fun.